CHRISTIAN FLESH

ENCOUNTERING TRADITIONS

Rumee Ahmed, Randi Rashkover, and Jonathan Tran

EDITORS

CHRISTIAN FLESH

PAUL J. GRIFFITHS

STANFORD UNIVERSITY PRESS
STANFORD, CALIFORNIA

Stanford University Press
Stanford, California

Printed in the United States of America on acid-free, archival-quality paper

Library of Congress Cataloging-in-Publication Data

Names: Griffiths, Paul J., author.
Title: Christian flesh / Paul J. Griffiths.
Description: Stanford, California : Stanford University Press, 2018. |
  Includes bibliographical references and index.
Identifiers: LCCN 2017058036 (print) | LCCN 2017061253 (ebook) |
  ISBN 9781503606753 (e-book) | ISBN 9781503606258 (cloth :alk. paper) |
  ISBN 9781503606746 (pbk. :alk. paper)
Subjects: LCSH: Flesh (Theology) | Human body—Religious
  aspects—Christianity.
Classification: LCC BT741.3 (ebook) | LCC BT741.3 .G76 2018 (print) |
  DDC 233/.5—dc23
LC record available at https://lccn.loc.gov/2017058036

Cover design: Rob Ehle
Cover art: *The Incredulity of Saint Thomas*, Caravaggio (ca. 1601–02). Sanssouci Picture Gallery, via Wikimedia Commons
Typeset by Bruce Lundquist in 10/14 Minion

For Lauren, with thanks

I am not here, touch me . . . that I may be here.

(Samuel Taylor Coleridge)

This hobble of being alive is rather serious.

(Thomas Hardy)

On the surface of it, the lover wants the beloved.
This, of course, is not really the case.

(Anne Carson)

Ille est verus dominus qui nihil a nobis quaerit.

(Augustine)

CONTENTS

PREFACE

In this book I offer a speculative theological depiction of human flesh in general and Christian flesh in particular. I write as a Catholic theologian who has in mind the deliverances of the teaching Church on the matters I write about; sometimes those deliverances surface, more often they don't, but they remain a constant informing presence. I intend, principally, clarification and speculative extension of the grammar of Christian thought and talk about human flesh. That purpose entails a deep unlikelihood that all the speculative positions I entertain and defend in this book are true. But since one of the theologian's tasks is to sketch patterns of thought and argument that grow from orthodox Christianity but are not (yet) part of it, that isn't a problem. Theology should be, first and last, about and responsive to the triune LORD who is its principal topic; it should then seek to be interesting; it is no part of the Catholic theologian's remit to be right.

I build here upon positions taken in earlier works, specifically *Intellectual Appetite* (2009), my commentary on the Song of Songs (2011), and my eschatological treatise *Decreation* (2014). I've learned a good deal from criticisms of those works, and have modified some of the positions entertained in them and dropped others. But in many cases, the positions offered in this book have roots in and presuppose sketches and arguments given in more detail in those earlier works, and for this reason I refer readers to them.

The method adopted here is direct and simple. It's grammatical: I attempt to write what can be written about human flesh using the lexicon and syntax provided by (a particular construal of) the Christian theological tradition. There are a few arguments in the book, but mostly it's a depiction of what might reasonably, if speculatively, be taken as well-formed utterances of a Christian sort about human flesh—and, concomitantly, a depiction and rejection of ill-formed utterances about that topic. Apart from fairly detailed engagement with some passages of Scripture, I largely eschew explicit engagement with texts from the Christian archive in pursuing these purposes. That's not because I despise such texts, or think there's nothing to be learned from them. Quite the reverse. Much of what I've written here is stimulated by what I've read from the archive, and there are, as the knowledgeable reader will easily see, many echoes of, disagreements with, and affirmations of what's to be found there. I choose not to quote or engage in exegesis mostly because the lines of a sketch are easily obscured by doing that, and what I hope for is a clear line. Proceeding principally by way of exegesis often, perhaps typically, derails theology by devolving theological argument and theological-grammatical sketch into recursive exegetical debate about how to read Thomas or Augustine or Barth or von Balthasar or . . . Those debates have their place; Christian theology can't do without them. But there's also a place for theology done in the mode offered here, and there is, it seems to me, in the anglophone Catholic world, a special reason for writing as I write here. That reason is that anglophone Catholic theologians aren't very good at theology and aren't very good at English. (Most Catholic theologians who think they are writing in English are hag-ridden by Latin and German and French, the Western languages of weight for the tradition, and so write something that isn't quite English, a Catholic hybrid of a rebarbative sort.) I include myself in both these criticisms. Improvements are possible, but they won't happen unless the task is faced directly, as I try and fail to do here. I had these points forcibly put to me by Tony Kelly in a bar in Melbourne in the (Australian) winter of 2014, and he's right; he's among the few anglophone Catholic theologians who do write theology in English.

Some conventions to note: LORD, uppercased, represents the divine name. When I use "god," I lowercase it, initial and all, unless I'm quoting someone else who doesn't. The reasons for this are provided in *Decreation*. I quote and elaborate upon Scripture always and only in the Latin of the *Nova Vulgata*. The justification for this is given, over-elaborately, in my "Which Are the Words of Scripture?" (*Theological Studies*, 2011). I provide no notes, whether foot- or end-. For readers who'd like to track down the texts I write about (there aren't many of them), I provide enough information in my text to make that easily possible. The (few) translations from nonscriptural works not composed in English are my own. And for the grateful acknowledgment of intellectual debt, there's the list of works consulted at the end of the book. More than that would detract from the book's method and purpose, betray my own lack of erudition, and very likely hew to an intellectually bankrupt and un-Christian understanding of intellectual property. I do provide, in the text, parenthetical references to numbered sections of this book, in which a point made in one place is developed in more detail in another, or in which useful background for understanding a point made in one place is given in another.

Lastly, about pronouns. "We" means one of three things: you and me, reader, the two of us working together; or, we Christians—you may not be one, and if you're not you can eavesdrop; or, we human beings. "You" picks out the one reading these words now. "I" indicates the one writing these words now. I don't use pronouns for the LORD, but do for Jesus, gendered masculine. And for the rest I follow ordinary English conventions.

ACKNOWLEDGMENTS

My principal debts in writing this book are to those who formed and instructed me in such a way that I could write it, and to those who were kind enough to read and comment on the manuscript at one or another stage of its composition. Among the first group, Aurelius Augustinus, Blaise Pascal, John Henry Newman, and Simone Weil are the most important. The second group includes, in alphabetical order, and with apologies to anyone I've forgotten, Carole Baker, Brendan Case, Lucila Crena, Derek Jeffreys, Philip Porter, Kavin Rowe, Evan Sandsmark, Kevin Schilbrack, and Carol Zaleski. I'm indebted, too, for conversations about some of the topics treated in the book, to Del Kiernan-Lewis, Jean-Luc Marion, Christian Moevs, and Rachel Teubner. A seminar discussing a draft at the University of Virginia in March 2017 was stimulating and helpful; my thanks are due to Chuck Mathewes for making that event possible, and to the faculty and doctoral students of that university's Department of Religion for participating in it. I learned, too, from Alexander Pruss's response to my comments on his book *One Body* (2013) in a symposium published in *Roczniki Filozoficzne* in 2015; that discussion informs and underlies the discussion of caresses in this book. Lauren Winner deserves special thanks for her generosity with time, conversation, and comment; I've learned a great deal from her. I don't mean, in acknowledging the help of these people, to implicate them in the views expressed and argued for in this book. They've helped me to be clearer about those views, and to argue for them better; that is all. The responsibility for any error of fact, judgment, interpretation, or argument is mine alone. I'm also grateful to Stanford University Press for publishing the book in its "Encountering Traditions" series, and especially to Emily-Jane Cohen for making the process so smooth and expeditious, and for offering good advice. The Press's two anonymous reviewers of the manuscript provided incisive and helpful comments, which have considerably improved the book.

CHRISTIAN FLESH

1 FLESH DEVASTATED

HUMAN FLESH, like all other flesh, is neither what it could be nor what it should be. It suffers and dies; is subject to disease from within and wounds from without; and finds itself in an apparently uncaring world to which it feels itself unnecessary. It is a disappointment to itself, and the care and maintenance of that disappointment require unremitting and debilitating effort. Christians take this state of things to be among the effects of a primordial cataclysm, a fall from order and harmony into chaos and decay. Once, human flesh was not like this, and eventually it will again not be like this. Others may eschew any general causal account, while agreeing that the flesh's agonies and disappointments are real; or they may offer causal accounts different from and sometimes incompatible with those belonging to Christianity, seeing, for example, fleshly suffering as an evolutionary spandrel, or as an epiphenomenon of desire. But there's wide agreement that flesh gives cause for lament, as there also is about what those causes are—suffering, decay, and death principal among them. Buddhists provide a particularly lively and precise analysis of this triad.

This book's first part depicts, with a Christian eye, human flesh as it now is—lively, erotic, haptic, suffering, condemned to death. That is the horizon for devastated flesh. Within that horizon, flesh is here distinguished from body as animate from inanimate (1.1) and is shown as constituted by the receipt and gift of touch (1.2), as at once bounded and porous (1.3), as ecstatically erotic (1.4), and as fragile (1.5).

1.1   Flesh and Body

Flesh is living body. Bodies without life are matter extended in spacetime, perhaps exiguously or discontinuously, but still extended; inanimate things are bodies *simpliciter*. Fleshly bodies, because they're bodies, are also matter extended in spacetime; they differ from other bodies in being alive. That's what makes them bodies of flesh. The history of a body of flesh is the history of a life. Its principle of organization, what makes it the fleshly body it is and not some other, is the principle of a life. Its boundaries, temporal and spatial, are the boundaries of a life.

—But isn't this a merely stipulative definition, inadequate to the use of "flesh" and "body" in ordinary English as well as in Christian talk? Aren't both words sometimes used to mark a value rather than as a description, and "flesh" usually a negative one? John writes, in his Gospel, *Spiritus est, qui vivificat, caro non prodest*—it's the Spirit who gives life, but the flesh produces nothing; and Paul writes, in Romans, "If you live according to the flesh (*secundum carnem*) you'll die; but if by the Spirit you put the body's works (*opera corporis*) to death, you'll live."

—Yes; but against that, *verbum caro factum est*: it's flesh that the Word becomes, and flesh that's offered as a means to eternal life. The Word becomes flesh, but the Church is Christ's body; living according to the flesh is opposed to living according to the Spirit, but Christ's flesh, when eaten, gives the gift of immortality; "incarnation" is a flesh-word (from *caro*), but is as likely as not to be rendered into English as "embodiment." There's no deep consistency in the use of these words among Christians or speakers of English. Sometimes they're interchangeable and sometimes not; sometimes one or the other carries value, and sometimes not. "Flesh," here, for the sake of clarity and consistency, always means "living body," with no value added. "Body," unmarked, means anything extended in timespace that doesn't live, also with no value added. The distinction between what lives and what doesn't is one of importance. It's useful to have a clear and consistent lexical usage to mark it, even if such clarity and consistency is stipulatively clearer and cleaner than the general Christian (or English) usage.

Christians say that what makes a body live is its soul. According to that usage, to say that a body lives is exactly to say that it is ensouled, animate; that word contains the Latin *anima*, which is ordinarily rendered "soul" in English.

All fleshly bodies, therefore, are ensouled: wherever there's flesh, there's also a soul. At a minimum, "soul" serves as a linguistic marker for whatever it is that permits a body to live, whatever it is that animates a body and thereby makes it flesh rather than body.

Most of the time it's easy enough to distinguish what lives from what doesn't without specifying just what it is that makes a living thing live. Distinguishing what lives from what doesn't, flesh from body, comes, for humans, easily and early, mostly by osmosis supplemented, when needed, by explicit catechesis. It happens, for the most part, as with all sortals, by considering particular things in light of paradigmatic cases. Trees and humans and snakes and birds and spiders all, obviously enough, live; rocks and stars and houses and fire and light all, almost equally obviously, don't. Encounters with new things in the world lead to assessment in terms of these clear cases, and then decision as to whether this, whatever it is, lives or doesn't. Ordinarily, there's no difficulty and no need for precision or abstraction in defining what it is that makes a body live.

Sometimes, however, there is a difficulty. Sometimes it's not clear to averagely skilled users of English whether to say of something they come across that it lives or doesn't. There are things that seem in some respects machinelike and therefore nonliving, but in other respects living, as when a computer converses in apparently reasonable ways. Or there are things such as self-replicating crystals that seem in some respects mineral-like, but are also self-moving and therefore perhaps living. And intuitions about when vegetable matter ceases to live—when it moves from (living) apple flesh, say, to rotting apple corpse— vary widely. Many, perhaps most, speakers of English are likely to say that the pips in an apple core they're eating aren't alive; but, when asked to notice that those pips might grow into a tree if planted, may revise their opinion.

For the most part, though, and most of the time, difficult cases and their concomitant criterial problems don't arise. It's ordinarily only when philosophy is done that criterial and definitional questions arise, and when they do they're difficult to resolve. But the criterial problem is almost entirely epistemic; it's not that there aren't good conceptual ways of distinguishing the living from the nonliving; it's rather that the ordinary ways of doing that sometimes fail to provide help in making decisions about whether some particular thing lives or doesn't, is flesh or body.

Flesh, as living body, comes in kinds corresponding to the kinds of living things, whatever those turn out to be. There's plant flesh, insect flesh, fishy flesh, avian flesh, and so on, as well as human flesh. It's not clear to what extent the ordinary, schoolbook classifications of living things into kinds (kingdom-phylum-class-family-genus-species) pick out natural kinds, kinds of things that exist, that is, independently of our acts of classifying them. They may exist in that way, but it's not obvious that they do. What is clear is that, for example, sorting living things according to similarity of genome yields different classifications than does sorting them by similarity of form. And those are not the only possible ways of sorting them. Our schoolbook classifications of living things are therefore best thought of as devices of convenience. It's not clear whether they are indeed anything more than that, and for most purposes, nothing much hinges on the question. Christians, certainly, need be wedded neither to broadly Aristotelean morphological classifications of living things, nor to genomic ones, even though both are usable and useful for particular purposes.

There are similar occasional difficulties of decision about what counts as human. Formal definitions are easy: theologically, a living thing is human if and only if it belongs to the kind that numbers among its members the human nature of Jesus. If it does, then the double-natured person Jesus Christ died for it; and if it doesn't, then he didn't. But this definition won't always yield an easy decision about whether this or that fleshly creature meets the case, as Christian difficulties (imaginary and actual) in deciding who (or what) may be baptized show. Alternatively, it's possible stipulatively to specify that a living creature is human if and only if its genome is of a certain sort; but that stipulation has the same drawback as the theological one, which is that there are some cases in which it's difficult to tell whether a fleshly creature has or lacks the appropriate genome. If, as is evident, members of what are ordinarily taken, genomically, to be one species, can breed with members of another, producing such things as wolvogs and mules, then the genomic criterion yields no easy decision about how to classify such things. The same is true of morphological definitions. This difficulty applies, too, to human interbreedings, of which there's decisive genetic evidence (*homo sapiens* with *homo neanderthalensis*, for example). Again, though, it's ordinarily possible to do what's needed, which is to determine without difficulty whether this or that living thing ought be thought of as human. In cases where there's real difficulty, the proper Christian response is one of relaxed generosity: if faced with flesh that there's first-blush reason to think human (to think, among other things, that Jesus died for it), the flesh in question is best treated as human—and therefore baptized—until there's decisive reason to conclude that it isn't. Better to mistake a nonhuman for a human than a human for a nonhuman.

1.2 Haptic Flesh

Flesh—all flesh, not just human flesh—has a double mode of interacting with the world in which it finds itself. The first is by touching other flesh, and the second by touching inanimate bodies. The two modes of interaction are always different in the order of being and usually different in the order of seeming. That is, the difference is real, whether or not it's apparent; touching (animate) flesh really differs from contacting (inanimate) body, and it usually also seems different.

When lovers kiss or caress they touch one another's flesh; when dogs nudge human hands with their noses, flesh touches flesh; so also when gardeners bury their noses in blowsy begonia blooms, when lions close their jaws on gazelles' napes, and when mosquitoes suck human blood. These are all fleshly exchanges ranging in kind from the caress to the blow, from the orgasmic embrace to the wounding that brings death. Such touches aren't accidental to flesh. Without them there's no flesh. It's only in being caressed and wounded by other flesh that flesh is given, as gift, the capacity itself to caress and wound. For mammalian flesh, to which human flesh belongs, the flesh-constituting gift exchange begins in the womb and ends only when death makes flesh into corpse. Not all fleshly touch is a caress: few humans reach adulthood without blows, injuries, and wounds, fleshly touches that turn flesh temporarily into an object transfixed by force. The caress provides flesh with the capacity to caress, and the blow gives it the capacity to wound. Fleshly capacity to touch other flesh is received without remainder as gift, even if the gift is often violent in this devastated world. Without the fleshly touch of others, flesh rapidly becomes body: it dies.

Flesh also interacts with the world by way of simple contact with inanimate bodies. This mode of interaction, omnipresent though it is (human flesh, once out of the womb, is always in contact with inanimate bodies, and necessarily so), is less important than fleshly touch for the constitution of flesh as flesh. Nonliving bodies neither caress nor wound, and therefore don't give the distinctive fleshly gift of being able to do those things. The pen between the fingers, the wood of the desk under the hand, the soft cotton of the undershirt next to the skin, the chair's cushion resisting the pressure of the buttocks—none of these is fleshly touch. In the order of being, contact between (animate) flesh and (inanimate) bodies is different in kind from fleshly touch, at least as different as the meeting of two solid bodies from the interpenetration of two gases.

This difference is also usually, but not infallibly, evident in the order of seeming. That is, tactile exchanges with flesh ordinarily seem different than do contacts with bodies. Stepping barefoot on a slug prompts a different response than does stepping barefoot on a sharp stone, and not just because one is soft and the other hard. Flesh acknowledges flesh differently than it does body. Similarly, a lover's slap on the cheek prompts a different response than does a similarly forceful blow from a pebble falling by chance from scree above. The one is a caress that may also be construed as a blow; the other is mere contact. They seem different as well as being different. They provide different things. This isn't to say that how things seem is also how they are. Flesh is sometimes caressed in ways that seem like mere contact, as when human flesh is involuntarily pressed into intimacy on the London Underground or the Chicago El; and flesh is sometimes contacted in ways that begin to seem like a caress, as when a zephyr strokes the skin. But for the most part, there's a good-enough match between the orders of being and seeming in matters of touch.

Contacts with inanimate bodies provide flesh with something essential, even if nothing flesh-constituting. They give the flesh what all bodies have, which is locatedness. Fleshly contacts with the inanimate provide flesh a place in timespace, a here-now-ness that is a defining characteristic of everything extended in timespace. There are various modes of locatedness, some of them puzzling because they seem to be (and perhaps are) discontinuous or exiguously thin; most of these modes of locatedness belong to bodies rather than to flesh, but it's possible that some also belong to flesh. If, for instance, angels and demons (who are fallen angels) have flesh, which is a claim disputed among Christians, then it's likely that their flesh is capable of discontinuous location in these ways; and Jesus's ascended flesh is simultaneously available eucharistically in widely dispersed places, and thus capable of a kind of spatiotemporal discontinuity.

Human flesh is, then, brought into being and maintained as flesh by touch from other flesh; and it's given its place in a spatiotemporally extended world by constant contacts with bodies. Without these tactile exchanges, there is no flesh; with them, flesh is. These are its fundamental and characteristic modes of interacting with the world: flesh touches and is touched, contacts and is contacted. These interactions are what makes flesh flesh and what gives it its place in a world.

—But how can it be that flesh is discriminated from body by the fact that it lives, and yet also that flesh is constituted as flesh only by its fleshly connections with other flesh? Doesn't this mean that living bodies isolated from all other flesh by accident or experiment, taken, perhaps, by scientists or aliens and placed in a sterile, inanimate environment, would become at once flesh and not? Flesh because it yet lives; and not-flesh because it's without the touch of other flesh, which is necessary for flesh to come to be flesh and continue to be flesh?

—Yes. But a distinction is necessary. Since the beginning of things, no flesh has come into being without touch. This is obvious in the case of sexual reproduction in all its varieties. It's equally the case, even if not quite so obviously so, in nonsexual reproduction. Cellular division, for instance, by means of which (it might be said; though other accounts might also be given—there are interesting mereological difficulties here) new cells—new living things, new fleshly things—come to be, requires for its occurrence intimate fleshly touch as the wall of one cell stretches, expands, and opens to make way for another. Reproduction of plant flesh by way of seeds can be accounted for similarly. The seed comes to be as seed because of intimate fleshly contact with (other parts of) the plant of which it is a seed. It is a living thing waiting only upon appropriate external circumstance to grow. Touch by flesh, then, is requisite for flesh to come to be. The experiment of placing flesh in a flesh-free environment doesn't call this aspect of flesh's definition—as living, and as constituted by touch—into question. One way to characterize such experiments is to say that they move flesh gradually toward body, away from life, that is, and toward death. Aging does the same. As human flesh ages, it becomes more and more like body. It loses, progressively, the characteristics of life. Sequestering flesh from touches by other flesh has similar effects. Flesh so sequestered approaches body because not only its coming-to-be as flesh, but also its continuing-to-be as such requires that kind of touch. Sequestered flesh is, therefore, flesh because it lives, but also flesh on the way to body because it has been deprived of one among the several conditions for its continuation as flesh—namely, the caresses (and blows) given by other flesh.

There is one exception to the principles just laid down. Once, in the order of time, the cosmos, all that is, included no flesh. There were no living bodies in it. And then, again in the order of time, flesh came to be. That flesh, the flesh that came to be when and where there had been none, wasn't brought into being by fleshly touch. For Christians, and perhaps also for Jews and Muslims, it was brought into being by the inspiration of (inanimate) bodies, which is to say by the LORD's breathing into them. This is an instance of creation out of nothing:

it brings life from not-life. For pagan (that is, neither Christian nor Jewish nor Muslim) theorists, there is as yet no widely agreed account of how life emerged from what doesn't live, and attempts to understand and replicate the process by which this occurred, whatever it was, have not (yet) been successful. Christians and others agree, however, that there was a time when non-divine life was not, and that its coming to be can't be accounted for by appeal to any of the ways in which it multiplies once it already exists.

Flesh is haptic, which is to say that flesh touches and is touched, contacts and is contacted. Those activities are what make it flesh; they are constitutive and defining of it. "Haptic" is an English word derived from the Greek *haptikos*, "capable of touch/touchy." The word became English (and French, and German) only in the nineteenth century, and has been adopted by those who study the sense of touch physiologically and, to a lesser extent, by those who study, historically, the ways in which touch has been thought about and represented. In its technical physiological use, "haptic" embraces at least the following. First, proprioperception, which is the flesh's perception of position and motion—of its location in the world and movement from place to place therein: it seems like something to me as the door swings wide, a new vista of space opens, and my flesh resonates now to this new space and the configuration of objects in it, and not to the space occupied before, on the door's other side. Second, kinaesthesis, which is the fleshly sense of effort and tension in muscles, tendons, and joints accompanying movement: it feels, or can feel if I'm paying attention, like something to me when my thigh muscles bunch in getting up from a chair, and when my foot pronates in taking a step. Third, the feeling of pressure and temperature on the skin, as when my flesh responds, feelingly, to the low humidity and high temperature of an afternoon in the high Arizona desert. Fourth, the sensation produced by direct contact between skin and some object external to it, as when my shin makes harsh contact with a table's edge in a dark room, or when my lover's lips brush the back of my neck.

To call flesh haptic is to say that it places itself and is placed, feels itself and is felt, in all these ways. These modes of interaction with the world, animate and inanimate, are proper to it. This might suggest that fleshly interactions with the world are exclusively a matter of touch: that the other sensory modalities have nothing to do with it. This is partly right and partly not.

Human flesh does more than touch other flesh and other bodies. It sees, hears, smells, tastes, speaks, moves, and thinks. All these have fleshly components, and most do not, and perhaps cannot, occur in the absence of flesh.

Discarnate cognition is, from a Christian point of view, possible: the triune LORD does it, and so do discarnate souls, the separated souls in the intermediate state between death and resurrection. But they aren't, strictly speaking, human creatures because human creaturehood requires flesh, and so, definitionally, all properly human cognition has a fleshly component or concomitant.

Even when non-haptic activities occur along with the flesh, in the flesh, they're neither the flesh's characteristic activity (they may be performed by unfleshly beings, though such beings are by definition not human) nor does all flesh do them. Flesh can exist without seeing, hearing, thinking, and so forth. Human flesh is no less human flesh when the human whose flesh it is sleeps dreamlessly or is in a coma. Then, its only mode of interacting with the world is tactile. It's only when it cannot touch or be touched that it ceases to be flesh: then it is dead and has become body. Fleshly touch, whether the caress or the blow or something between, doesn't have to be experienced as such by those exchanging it in order to be what it is. Lovers entwined asleep in bed are touching one another's flesh even though it doesn't seem like anything to them to be doing it; a sleeping baby supported by its father's hand under its buttocks and with its breathing mouth next to his ear is being touched by flesh even though it's too deeply asleep for this to seem like anything to it; and those in coma whose hands are held, foreheads caressed, and flesh washed by others are touching and being touched, coma notwithstanding. The only thing that prevents fleshly touch is death. Many other things prevent the exercise of the other senses: human flesh can be blind, deaf, mute, and motionless without thereby ceasing to be human flesh.

In the ordinary Western classification of the senses, touch is one of five. It requires contiguity. It's not possible to touch something at a distance. To receive the caress or the wound, your flesh needs immediate connection to someone else's. The same is true for contacts with inanimate creatures: the chair needs to be in contact with the buttocks for sitting to occur, and the skin needs to be wetted by water in order to be washed. In the case of touch, the thing touched and the act of touching aren't, and can't be, spatially or temporally separated: caressing an absent lover isn't possible. All these things are also true of taste. It's not possible to taste something unless it's on the tongue, contiguous with the nerve endings there that trigger the phenomenon. Tasting at a distance, like caressing at a distance, is oxymoronic. If touching something is defined as immediate fleshly contact with that thing, for which contiguity is requisite, then taste is an instance of it; it's a kind of touching performed by the tongue.

Matters are more complex for sight, hearing, and smell. The objects of those senses—the things heard, seen, and smelled—are ordinarily distant from the flesh when heard, seen, and smelled. Not only that: it's usually difficult, and sometimes impossible, to see, hear, or smell something contiguous with the relevant sensory organ. It's difficult to see what's pressed up against your retina, to hear what's in your ear canal, or to smell what's up your nose. Those senses work best at some distance, and, therefore, with intermediaries between the fleshly sensory organs and the things they sense. Hearing, for example, requires, ordinarily, some vibration-capable medium (air, water, and so on) between the thing heard and the ear doing the hearing. Sight requires, similarly, intermediate light, and smell a medium capable of carrying the small particles of what's being smelled into the olfactory cavity. Acquaintances walk the hallway toward one another. They see one another coming, hear the distinctive fall of one another's feet on the floor, perhaps smell one another. But what they see, hear, and smell isn't yet contiguous with them. It may yet be yards away, and when they're up against one another, talking face to face, shaking hands, or giving an air kiss, they may no longer be able to see one another at all, and they hear and smell one another differently than they did at a distance.

There are difficulties here, however. Seeing, hearing, and smelling do require contiguity of a sort, and to the extent that they do, they're haptic. In order for the lover's flesh to be olfactorily available at a distance, there must be contiguity between some particles of those things and the olfactory nerves. That's a kind of contiguity, even if not one that directly connects the thing smelled to the olfactory organ. Similarly for the sound of the footfall, which requires some vibrating air to come into contact with receptors in the inner ear, and the look of the face, which needs contiguity between patterned light and the retina. These three senses therefore require, and are partly constituted by, the sense of touch. That they can do what they do—see, hear, and smell things at a distance—is made possible by the flesh, which is to say made possible by touch. Nonetheless, they're not exhaustively accountable by touch: what's seen, heard, and smelled at a distance is exactly the thing seen, heard, and smelled. That's not possible for touch: for that, contiguity is needed. It is conceptually possible, by stipulative definition, to subsume without remainder all senses into the tactile, but doing so requires the conclusion that what the lover smells isn't the beloved's sweat but rather particles in the nose; what the lover sees isn't the beloved's face, but rather patterns on the retina; and what the lover hears isn't the beloved's bootheels on the floor, but rather vibrations in the ear. That usage, however, isn't English and also not that of any natural language; the track along which it moves thought isn't one to be followed here, and so the distinction between sight, hearing, and smell, on the one hand, and touch and taste, understood as a kind of touch, on the other, is maintained. This usage provides a haptic fundament for sight, hearing, and smell, but doesn't reduce them to it. It also maintains the idea that flesh is fundamentally and essentially tactile, and that hearing, sight, and smell do not, for human creatures, work in the absence of flesh because of their irreducible tactile component.

Understanding human flesh as constitutively haptic has another important advantage. It permits easy and productive characterization of what human flesh has in common with other kinds of flesh. Indo-Tibetan Buddhist thought is helpful here. It tends to classify living things according to the number of senses they have, and to arrange them in a hierarchy according to that number. At the bottom of the hierarchy come living things with only one sense, called *sparśa* in Sanskrit, which can be rendered "touch" with reasonable adequacy. Living things higher up the hierarchy add senses: some can smell and taste as well as touch; others can also see and hear; and others still add to these intellectual senses of various kinds (Buddhist theorists typically think that there are more than five senses). This view accords with and illuminates Christian thought about the hierarchy of being and pagan scientific classificatory thought about the kinds of living things there are. Like both those ways of thinking, the Buddhist systems see and show that what distinguishes living from nonliving things is their capacity for touch. Animate bodies—bodies of flesh—are what they are because they can exchange fleshly touch with other such bodies. Unicellular organisms can do this, and only this: they interact with the world only in that way. The same is true for more complex single-sensed creatures like worms and viruses (if it's proper to think that viruses live; they are a nice instance of unclarity about the boundaries between the animate and the inanimate). Inanimate things, by contrast, however internally complex they may be, touch nothing: they have no *sparśa*, but merely come into contact with things. That's true of planets, stars, bodies of water and gas, and so forth. To be fleshly, this view shows, is exchangeable with being haptic, and with being alive. To lose life is to cease to be flesh and, thus, to cease being haptic.

This view makes sense, too, of the ordinary distinctions all human languages and social systems draw between what lives and what doesn't. Humans speak about and interact with living things differently than they do with nonliving things, and mostly think about those who don't recognize this distinction—

those who, for example, might take a hammer to the skull of a living dog with the same insouciance they'd use in breaking stones—as badly damaged. Judgments of this sort become more definitive the greater the similarity the living creature in question has to the one making the judgment: decapitating a bonobo seems different, and worse, to most humans than does swatting a mosquito, and that's largely because the bonobo seems more like humans than does the mosquito. That's not to say humans don't do things like decapitating bonobos with abandon. Slaughterhouses show that we do. But it is to say that a stonemason's shop seems to most to be very different from an abattoir, and does so exactly because the latter deals in flesh and the former does not. The difference between what lives and what doesn't is written deeply into every natural language and every legal system, and that's because languages and law recognize the difference that flesh makes, and attribute moral significance to that difference.

1.3   Flesh's Bounds

Flesh, in addition to being constituted by the contiguities of touch, is always self-contiguous. That is, it has no spatially separable parts. Its matter is always extended in space without breaks or gaps.

Consider what happens when part of a fleshly body's living matter is separated from it—a thief's hand is hacked off, a snake's skin is sloughed, a worm is sliced in two by the edge of a gardener's spade. In the first two cases, the separated matter at once, or almost at once, ceases, by dying, to be flesh, and the flesh from which it has been separated is reconfigured by the loss. That fleshly body continues to live, but now with different boundaries; what's been removed from it, however, doesn't continue to live, or not for long. The snake's loss of skin and the thief's loss of a hand don't alter the self-contiguity of their flesh by effecting spatial separation between their parts. But in the third case, that of the worm's flesh divided by the gardener's blade, something different may happen. It may be that each part remains alive as a self-sustaining and self-contiguous body of flesh, and that the two wriggle off in different directions, each to do, as a whole and self-sufficient worm, whatever it is that worms do. In this case, what was one self-contiguous body of flesh has become two. Something like this happens when cells divide.

Even in cases like this, the principle that a fleshly body is self-contiguous and can't be divided into spatially separated parts isn't called into question. A fleshly body's boundaries typically change over time, sometimes dramatically, but such a body doesn't and can't have separated parts of itself scattered around the cosmos. Matter removed from it can continue to exist in only three ways: as inanimate body (the ordinary case); as an independent body of flesh; and as part of another body of flesh, as when an organ is removed from your flesh and incorporated, still living, into the flesh of another. In none of these cases is that separated matter to be understood as separated flesh. That locution makes no sense. When a living kidney is in transit between donor and recipient, it's flesh in its own right, awaiting incorporation; it's not a piece of separated flesh.

A different account is needed for temporal parts. Christian orthodoxy requires that human bodies of flesh cease to be for a while, perhaps a very long while, consequent upon death, and that they are then resurrected as the same fleshly bodies they once were. The model here is the flesh of Jesus. That flesh ceased to be between Good Friday afternoon and Easter Sunday morning because Jesus was dead, which means exactly that there was no flesh on the cross after he died there, no flesh transported between cross and tomb, and no flesh in the tomb because there was only a *corpus*, a corpse-body, there between Good Friday afternoon and Easter Sunday morning. But then, on Sunday morning, that *corpus*, that congeries of inanimate matter, became flesh, and in so becoming was resurrected as the same fleshly body that had died thirty hours or so earlier. Similarly (not identically) for others: if hope is fulfilled, all human bodies of flesh will be resurrected for salvation: those bodies will exist again after a time of nonbeing. This means that fleshly bodies can, and perhaps ordinarily do, have separated temporal parts: they can exist for a while, cease to exist, and then exist again. There are conceptual difficulties that get in the way of understanding this, among which the most pressing is the question of what makes a resurrected fleshly body the same as the fleshly body it was before its death. Whatever is to be made of these difficulties—and they have deep interest—all that's necessary here is to note them, and to emphasize that Christian flesh (and perhaps all human flesh; perhaps, even, all flesh *simpliciter*) does have temporally separated parts: it comes to be at a time, continues for a while, ceases to be with death, and then comes to be again with resurrection.

Spatial self-contiguity entails boundaries. Every fleshly body has them. In mammals they're constituted (mostly) by skin and hair. Where skin and hair end, roughly speaking, is where mammalian bodies of flesh end; everything external to that skin is also external to that flesh. Nonhuman fleshly bodies also have boundaries—those of a tree's flesh, for example, are ordinarily given by its bark—and they too are constituted as the kinds of flesh they are by the kinds of touch and contact they exchange with fleshly bodies external to themselves. (Plants, for instance, are typically capable of photosynthetic contact with light that is important to their constitution as a peculiar kind of flesh; that kind of contact is alien to human flesh.) These boundaries are not constant. All fleshly bodies are capable of growth and shrinkage, of loss of parts by splitting and accrual of new parts by grafting and in other ways.

Bounded though bodies of flesh are, they're also porous to the world in which they find themselves. They don't only touch it and have contact with it; they also take it into themselves and disgorge their by-products, and sometimes also parts of themselves, into it. Ingestion and leakage, that is, are properly characteristic of flesh: it receives the world into itself and gives itself outward into that same world. There's a constant systole and diastole of exchange with the world without which no fleshly body can live. Boundedness doesn't entail monadic isolation; in its fleshly form it requires exchange.

In the human case, leakage into the world includes blood, sweat, tears, piss, shit, semen, milk, and breath. Some of these leakages are regular and frequent, and some are irregular and occasional. Many other bodily fluids and secretions are leaked or otherwise exuded in times of wounding or illness. These fluids find their way through the integument of the skin, or through its openings; their doing so provides a deep and visceral sense of the fragility of the flesh, of its necessary intimacy with the world beyond its bounds, and of that world's saturation with fleshly effluvia. Falstaff lards the earth with his sweat; and almost every square meter of it is saturated with human blood. Sometimes, too, involuntary fleshly leakages produce fear and shame, as happens when adults bleed or urinate or vomit in public; sometimes they produce delight, as when lovers exchange bodily fluids—the mother gives milk to her child and the lover semen to his beloved. The same is true of the leakages of others: those of beloveds can delight, but out-of-place fleshly effluvia—blood or semen or shit where local norms suggest they ought not be—can revolt.

Ingestion is as frequent and necessary to flesh as leakage, and it too provides the flesh with a strong sense of its porosity to the world. Mammalian lungs suck air; plants eat light; whales, open-mouthed, harvest phytoplankton; bats, sonar-guided, suck in bloodsucking mosquitoes; sharks, blood-inflamed, ingest even their own flesh when wounded; and humans eat often and indiscriminately, finding a high proportion of the world's things suitable for ingestion. Human infants and small children typically have to be catechized and disciplined in order to constrain the range of their gastronomic tastes. All flesh lives by ingestion, and this, like the necessity and frequency of its leakages, relates it constantly and intimately to the world external to its boundaries. For most flesh—for all of it, in fact, other than most plants—ingestion is largely of still-living or recently dead flesh. This is as true for vegans and vegetarians as for omnivores, because the plant flesh they prefer lives no less than animal flesh. It may even be that a higher proportion of a vegetarian diet is of living flesh than is that of omnivores—much of the latter's diet is likely to be made up of safely, if recently, dead animal bodies, while the former are happy to eat still-living plant flesh.

This preference on the part of fleshly bodies for other fleshly bodies when eating means that the economy of the flesh is one of slaughter (5.1); it also means that there's an order-of-being intimacy that binds all flesh together in a way that flesh is not bound to inanimate body. In encountering flesh, humans are encountering something that may be edible—and something that may eat them. That's much less often the case when humans encounter inanimate bodies. Those are less likely to be edible, and they never eat us even when they kill us in other ways. This fleshly economy of killing and eating certainly obtains in the order of being. It's a fundamental feature of the devastated world. But that economy also has a phenomenal effect. Most humans, most of the time, feel themselves intimate with fleshly bodies in a way they do not with inanimate ones, and the need for and nature of ingestion is a concomitant of the bloody economy of the flesh, which is to say of the constant exchange of flesh with world by the ingestion of other flesh. The pet rock is an aberration in much the same way that the rock served for dinner would be. Each is an attempt to bring something inanimate into the economy of the flesh.

Breaching the bounds of fleshly bodies doesn't occur only by way of leakage and ingestion. It also occurs by way of symbiosis. Within the integument of skin that marks the bound between a particular instance of human flesh and the world in which it lives—inside human flesh, that is, rather than outside it—live many nonhuman creatures. In the gut and mouth, for example, there are always many thousands of microbes living, and the same is true, though in lower concentration, in most other parts of human flesh. As well as these constant companions, human flesh harbors from time to time many other living things within its flesh: viruses, bacteria, larger parasites, babies, and so on. Sometimes these visitors kill or sicken; sometimes their presence passes unnoticed; and sometimes it contributes to flourishing, or is a cause for delight, as when a woman bears a wanted child. All this is symbiosis, and is very different from participation in the economy of the flesh by slaughter or ingestion, and not only because it isn't predicated upon death but is instead a matter of the mutually supportive caress. It's also different because it rarely has phenomenal effects: symbiotic fleshly intimacies fall very largely below the horizon of awareness, which means that they have little or no effect upon the human sense of what it is to be a body of flesh. Fleshly symbiosis is a constant feature of the human mode of being in the world; but with the exception of pregnancy and some instances of infestation by large parasites, it is not a feature of the order of fleshly seeming.

The spatial boundedness of fleshly bodies doesn't only separate them from and relate them to bodies other than themselves. It also places them in a world of such bodies, the vast majority of which they will never touch because they are too distant for contiguity. Some of these untouchables can be seen or heard or smelled; it's even possible for flesh constituted to have sensory connections of these kinds with bodies that no longer exist—you can, for example, see heavenly bodies that long ago ceased to exist because of the time taken by their light to reach your eyes; and, more mundanely, a pistol shot is heard an eyeblink after it's seen because of the difference between the speeds at which light and sound travel on a planet like this one. But most of the bodies, animate and inanimate, to be found in the world lie beyond even these possibilities of sense, and all the more beyond the possibility of touch. If the sphere of bounded fleshly experience is limited to what's touchable, then it belongs properly and essentially to the flesh to be placed in a world mostly inaccessible to itself, a world that lies always beyond its reach. Being flesh exactly means to have most of the world given externally to the flesh, projected on a visual, auditory, and olfactory screen apart from the flesh—a screen that resonates and is redolent with distance.

These are truths in the order of being. They indicate something important about the relations between flesh and world. They show that human fleshly intimacies are extraordinarily local because they require contact with skin. To attend to and interact with what lies beyond the skin's touch is, necessarily, to leave the flesh behind and enter into unfleshly exchanges with the world. It's not that these unfleshly exchanges don't require flesh for their occurrence: distant and possibly now nonexistent stellar arrays remain invisible without eyes, which are flesh. But it is to say that seeing these stars is an unfleshly event. When a toddler reaches for the stars, can't grasp them, and is disappointed, she's apprehending something of great importance, something that is, to most adults, so deeply written upon the flesh as to be unremarkable but which in reality informs every moment of fleshly existence. It is that to be a body of flesh is to be in a world of lack, a world that calls us to fleshly intimacy with it but that at the same time denies that intimacy to us.

Truths in the order of being, however, are not usually straightforwardly also truths in the order of seeming and knowing. How it seems to bodies of flesh to find themselves in a world, therefore, varies enormously. But for human flesh some generalizations can be offered. The first is that it is common for human flesh to feel itself *de trop* in the face of a world of vast extent that is in principle beyond fleshly intimacy, and that often seems to exhibit no interest in or concern for the flesh it does not touch. This aspect of how it seems to be flesh in a world is more prevalent and more pressing for those who've lived since the invention of devices (microscopes, telescopes, and so on) that permit sight (but not touch) of infinitesimally small and ungraspably large things, and to know that these are what's being seen. It's hard to think, and harder still to feel, that these things have anything to do with human flesh, positively or negatively. To what's seen in the Hubble Telescope or in the latest image broadcast from a Jupiter-orbiting spacecraft, human flesh is irrelevant: they are what they are, have been what they have been, and will be what they will be, without respect to human flesh and its interests; and that sense of the state of things can be, for humans, depressing, terrifying, and exhilarating. What it cannot easily do is produce a sense of intimacy with the world. The more we meditate on it, the more alien to human flesh the world seems. And while this sense of the world is common and deep to those who've lived since the seventeenth century, it's not absent before that. For those often faced with the open seas, the wide deserts, or the dark forests on this small planet, something of the same almost inevitably happens. A voyage on a small boat across the Atlantic or a week's hike in the deserts of the American Southwest will go a long way toward making those who do such things seem to themselves *de trop* to the world, and the world vastly excessive to and profoundly uncaring about them. Seemings and understandings such as this have the added and important feature of being adequate to some important truths about the world in the order of being: the world is in fact radically excessive to human flesh; and human flesh is in fact largely irrelevant to what goes on in the world. That's not all there is to say about the relations between human flesh and the untouchable world it finds itself in. But anything else that might be said shouldn't contradict these truths.

Human flesh's spatial boundedness is matched by its temporal bounded-ness. To be located in space is also to be located in time, and this is as true of human flesh as of every other body, animate and inanimate. The flesh's skin, which is its boundary, marks not only the space it occupies but also the time it takes. There was a time when any particular human body of flesh was not, and there will be a time when once again it is not, and then again, accord-ing to the Christian view of things, a time when it will be—the progression is from conception to death to resurrection. Human flesh is timebound to just the same extent that it is spacebound. That much isn't controversial. Neither is the thought that whatever account of time is the correct one in the order of being, there's a great deal of it, and the segment of it taken up by human flesh, severally or collectively, is an infinitesimally small part of the whole. According to the now standard (though not undisputed) view of time's passage as a linear, calendrically measurable series with a beginning, there may have been twelve billion years of it since the beginning, with more yet to come. No human fleshly body has lived more than a hundred and twenty years or so, which aptly illus-trates the insignificance of the time human flesh takes.

According to a Christian view, there is no passage of time in the order of being; the distended linearity of time is an artifact of the fall and will be set right when all things are as they should be and creatures participate according to their kinds and capacities in the circumincessive eternality of the Holy Trin-ity. On that view, human fleshly existence is still temporally bounded, but its very temporality relates it atemporally to the LORD who is not bound by time, and to whom all creatures are always fully present. On both accounts, flesh is definitively temporally bounded, now and always.

The first moment of a human fleshly body's spatiotemporal existence is its conception, which ordinarily occurs as the result of the uniting of sperm and egg in a woman's womb. This is when the coming together of two bodies of flesh (sperm and egg, each alive and each capable of being individuated) brings into being a new one, a previously inexistent human body of flesh. (There are some difficulties here because a fertilized egg, in the week or so between its fertiliza-tion and its implantation in the uterine wall, is capable both of division—which produces identical twins—and merging—which produces chimeras; twinning and merging are not properties ordinarily taken to belong to human flesh, and there is therefore a reasonable, though not decisive, case for saying that a previ-ously nonexistent human fleshly body doesn't come to be until these things are no longer possible, which is to say at about the eighth day after fertilization.)

Every human body of flesh begins in this way, is subsequently born in one way or another into the timespaced world, and continues in that world for a brief span until it comes to an end in death, at which time it ceases to be flesh and becomes a corpse, an assemblage of inanimate body parts.

That's the ordinary spatiotemporal career of a body of flesh: brought to be without its consent or involvement, as gift (or curse); thrown into a vastly extended world in which timespace extends untouchably and incomprehensibly before, behind, and around it; subject from its unasked beginning to damage from without and decay from within; and rapidly approaching its own end as flesh by the loss of life that is in it.

As with space, so with time: what's given to flesh in the order of being may appear to particular bodies of flesh in varied ways, and with similar variegation to the same flesh at different times and places in its temporal career. Both time and space are experienced unevenly—as bunched, folded, stretched, repetitive, cyclical, gridded, and much more—by all flesh. The three-year-old's sense of the spacetime of a long summer afternoon is different from the adult athlete's sense of the timespace of her one-hundred-meter sprint, and each is different from the timespace sense of someone listening to Messiaen's "Quatuor pour la fin du temps" for the hundredth time or that of someone repetitively piece-working on an assembly line—as those, too, differ from one another. The regular and evenly spaced passage of time, measured by the clock tick or sidereal motion, is a useful fiction of measurement, rarely reflected with regularity in the texture of fleshly spatiotemporal experience.

There's similar variety in the sense that particular fleshly bodies have of the extent of time, and of their unasked and brief place in it. Some feel as heavy the burden of time's oceans before and after their own taking of time. They feel temporally *de trop*, as well as spatially so. This sense of things is likely more pressing for those who know of the twelve billion or so years of time before they came to be. Others, it seems, have no lively sense of this, even if they know it to be the case. This can be so for those inclined, as all children are, toward solipsism; such flesh, even if it gives notional assent to the fact of the clock ticks that preceded its coming to be and will follow its ceasing to be, doesn't find its sense of what it's like to be a spatiotemporal creature much affected by that notional assent. In extreme cases of this kind, it may seem that the only kind of time there is or can be is one's own: that time came to be with oneself and will end with one's absence—if one's absence is conceivable, which for the solipsist it is not. Others may sit experientially loose to time's calendrical passage because their sense of time is given them primarily by the nonidentical cyclical repetitions of the liturgy. This may often be true for Christians and Jews and others whose lives are ordered by liturgical observance; and there are secular forms of this time sense, too—the man whose life is ordered by baseball may find his time sense given largely by the rhythms and repetitions of the baseball season and the open-ended temporal structure of the game itself.

There are, however, some very widespread features of time's feel for human bodies of flesh. Most prominent among these—almost universal, probably, among those who live to be older than thirty or so—is the sense of approaching death, which, put temporally, is the sense that the texture of spatiotemporal existence for this flesh is moving toward its end, moving toward a line that cannot be crossed in the flesh. This aspect of the sense of time's passage belongs to the order of seeming, but it is also intimate with the order of being, in which there is no flesh that does not die.

1.4   Flesh's Eros

Human flesh, like all other flesh, is gift. Both that it is and what it is are given; it neither brings itself into being nor maintains itself in being. These states of affairs are simple and direct gifts, and they make human flesh essentially ecstatically erotic. To be given oneself as flesh is to be given oneself as intrinsically desirous of and delighting in fleshly intimacies with others—as standing outside oneself in seeking and responding to the flesh of others. The gift of flesh is given and received, among humans, principally by caress.

The first caress is given by mother to child in the womb; the second is given immediately upon birth as the mother receives her newborn; the third is that of nipple to mouth and breast to cheek as the infant, greedy for food, latches and sucks. That, anyway, is the ordinary story, a story that human flesh shares with most mammalian flesh. The story can be disrupted by technological intervention and by accident, among other things. But ordinarily, that's the way it goes.

Following those first caresses, the child is caressed by many other humans— family, friends, a widening circle as the child's sphere of activity expands and her interests and range of acquaintance bloom. Children are eager for caresses, and largely undiscriminating as to their source; they are likely to welcome caresses from all and sundry, human and nonhuman, and to return those caresses with passion. Children from birth to the age of five or so seem, often, to have the ingestion of the cosmos as their central purpose: anything and everything is worthy of the intimate oral caress. Their appetites for giving and receiving caresses are intense, omnidirectional, and reciprocal. That last term indicates that the child's caresses are prompted and made possible by the caresses of others. Those caresses, graceful gifts, are necessary conditions for the establishment of the child as flesh, which is to say as capable of caressing just and only because caressed. Without caresses from other humans, infants ordinarily die; and if, by some miracle, they live, they fail to flourish. Infants and children are, ordinarily, desperate in their search for the caress, which is to say also desperate in their desire to themselves be constituted as flesh. There are evolutionary biological reasons for this: such desire is a necessary condition for survival. There are also theological ones: the trinitarian economy includes flesh and, therefore, caresses. The triune LORD, in constituting flesh as a creature of the caress, constitutes it in the image and likeness of the incarnate LORD. Caresses are proper to the LORD as well as to fleshly creatures; and the caresses exchanged by creatures participate in those exchanged by the LORD with creatures—when human flesh seeks the kisses of the mouth, as it is shown to do at the beginning of the Song of Songs, it seeks, certainly, the kisses of human beloveds—the lover and the beloved in the Song are human—but it also, preveniently, seeks the LORD's kisses—the Song's beloved, panting for love, wants the LORD.

The erotic appetites of human flesh are, when compared with other mammalian flesh, underdetermined by genetic inheritance. Those human appetites are very largely plastic, as is evident by the baroque variety of behaviors found among humans in service of them. As Shakespeare's Troilus says to Cressida, in an ambiguous love speech in the third act of the play named after them, "This is the monstruosity in love, lady—that the will is infinite and the execution confined; that the desire is boundless and the act a slave to limit." The desire is boundless because human flesh can and does seek fleshly intimacy in an infinite number of ways; the act is a slave to limit because there isn't world enough or time to explore all these ways.

In infancy and childhood, erotic appetite is largely unrestricted and unfocused. With the coming of puberty, there is a new focus for ecstatic eros, because of the new possibility of procreation. When humans become capable of begetting children, usually sometime during the second decade of their lives, some of their erotic appetites are channelled toward kinds of fleshly intimacy not possible before, kinds that include copulative intimacy whose paradigmatic act is the ejaculation of semen by a man into a woman. This caress, together with its precursors and accompaniments, begins to be sought, knowingly or not, by many, perhaps most, human creatures not long after it becomes possible for them. But even when it's possible, and even when it's sought, it's implausible to think that all the fleshly intimacies sought by adolescents with one another are directed toward or ordered to copulative intimacies. When a fourteen-year-old pair, delighting in one another's company, begin to write sonnets confessing endless passion to one another and for one another, hymning, perhaps as the Song of Songs does, the beauties of various parts of their bodies ("your lips are like a crimson thread / and your mouth is lovely"), and affirming that their love is stronger than death and capable of overcoming all obstacles, it isn't obvious that the intimacies they seek from and with one another all have something to do with the copulative caress and should be assessed in terms of the relation they bear to it. What they want from one another is both vastly more and (often) vastly less than that.

It's more in the sense that their fleshly appetites for one another are in dramatic excess of the particular act that can produce children. They're as likely to be interested in one another's toes and breasts and buttocks, and especially in one another's eyes, as in their penises and vaginas—to be interested in every aspect and element of the beloved's flesh, and thereby to eroticize the whole. That's part of the import of the quotation from *Troilus and Cressida* already given: human fleshly desires are radically excessive to any particular caresses, even procreative ones. Humans are animals, of course; but human desire for fleshly intimacies is unlike that of other animals exactly in its excessive nature. What humans want by way of fleshly intimacy with one another goes far beyond the copulative caress. They want, for instance, to be face-to-face with their beloveds, to stare into the inscrutably dark pupils of their eyes, and to exchange open-mouthed kisses with them—and they want these things not just, or at all, because they're accompaniments of or ancillary to procreative caresses, but because they're more intimate than those, more expressive of the fundamental fleshly desire, which is to receive by way of the beloved's touch the gift of being loved and being a beloved—to be brought into being by touch, by the haptic flesh. Being eye to eye and lip to lip is at least as expressive of this desire as is being penis to vagina. It's easier to commercialize copulative intimacies, to bring them into the sphere of the pimp and the prostitute, than to do the same with the intimacy of the soulful gaze or the open-mouthed kiss. That's one sign of the difference, a difference of excess.

What the members of a loving couple want from each other may also be less than copulative intimacy, in the sense that they do not seek, and might reject if it becomes possible, precisely the act in which copulative intimacy consists. This might be for a variety of reasons: the intimacies of that fleshly act might be less delightful to them than the intimacies of other fleshly acts; they might want from one another kinds of continuing intimacy that they take copulation to preclude; and so on.

The upshot is that even when puberty has made procreative caresses possible, it's far from reasonable, prima facie, to think that all the fleshly intimacies sought by a postpubertal couple are to be assessed in terms of the relation they bear to those very particular caresses.

The unique (it seems) plasticity of human fleshly eros, which is evident in its radical and greedy openness to and desire for the flesh of others, is rapidly shaped and formed by catechesis provided in accord with local norms about fleshly caresses. Children, from infanthood onward, are given stern and repeated instruction in these matters by adults, instruction repeated and intensified by peers at every stage of development. This instruction has to do not only with the flesh and its possibilities, but also with those of gender, which term labels the locally normed expressions and signs of sexual identity. By puberty, this catechesis will have had its effects, both with respect to desire for the exchange of fleshly caresses and with respect to the kinds of caress actually exchanged. Expectations about the possibilities and nature of the flesh are by then in place, as are the beginnings of fleshly habits and habits of desire; and by the third decade of life, at the latest, these habits are typically deeply formed and beyond significant alteration. By then, the flesh's eros is what it is; there are only small possibilities for future change. Life is short, and habits run deep. Once flesh is scarified and overwritten by habit and local catechesis, much as linguistic capacity is when learning a mother tongue, not much will change later. What was plastic and ductile adopts a statue-like rigidity: fleshly tastes, like gait or accent, become effectively fixed. But even at this stage, there's no single configuration in which they're fixed. There are those who obsessively seek copulative intimacy with as many others as possible. There are those who eschew that kind of intimacy altogether, whether in favor of other caresses, or of none. And there are those whose repertoire of caresses is small and infrequently repeated, just as there are those with a wide repertoire, often and enthusiastically performed. Very conservatively, more than ninety percent of all caresses exchanged by adult humans have nothing obvious (in the order of seeming) and nothing in fact (in the order of being) to do with the copulative caress.

Human ecstatic fleshly eros is not directed only toward other human flesh. It's directed also toward nonhuman flesh: there are roses to smell, dogs to stroke, snakes to handle, trees to climb, grass to roll in, and, endlessly, plant and animal flesh to chew and swallow. In all these cases, human flesh's ecstatic eros is evident and active; it receives from these fleshly exchanges an intensi-fication and shaping of that eros in ways closely akin to the intensifications it receives from fleshly exchange with other humans. Human flesh finds itself in a world of nonhuman flesh with which it is also ecstatically eager to be intimate—even as it also finds itself under threat of danger and death by the presence of that flesh. Human flesh's eros is always modulated by a sense of its own fragility, and of the damage that can be done to it by the flesh of others, human and otherwise.

1.5   Flesh's Fragility

A sense of fragility is written deeply into human flesh, from its beginning. As soon as they're born, infants startle at loud noises (a possible threat) or when they're suspended over a void (a potential fall). That sense of fragility, that the world is dangerous to flesh, intensifies with time and experience. Infants learn, with apparent surprise, the boundaries of their own flesh, often by gumming and sucking it; they don't always exhibit pleasure at the sensations this yields. They learn, too, about the kinds of pain the world can bring to their flesh: rough ground cuts and bruises; hot things scald and blister; sharp things cut and bring blood; cold things freeze and goosebump; bees sting, ants bite; rain wets, sun burns; and the palms and fists and feet and teeth of other humans pummel and hurt. Few, even among the most privileged, reach their fifth year without undergoing the world's severe catechesis of pain in all these ways. The story of Prince Siddhartha, the Buddha-to-be who reaches young manhood without any sense of the flesh's fragilities because of the care with which his parents have sheltered him from them, is fabulously implausible. It gains its power from the sharpness of the relief into which it throws the omnipresence and intensity of quotidian human fleshly suffering inflicted from without, by the world in which it finds itself. Human flesh has its fragility impressed upon it daily, usually by its own pain, but also by its observation of the fleshly pains of others. Human flesh therefore inhabits the world guardedly, wearing a carapace of careful avoidance of the occasions of pain. Every caress is also a threat; every step also a danger.

The world not only wounds flesh from without; it also attacks it from within. One day breath comes easily, smoothly, and unthinkingly, and the next it's a struggle, punctuated by coughs and wheezes; one day the bowels empty as usual, producing faeces firm and well-shaped, and the next there's flux and pain and bloody diarrhoea; one day the flesh is free of pain, walking the world without care or thought, and the next there's pain in the joints, insupportable and sudden; one day the flesh is cool and happy, unaware of its temperature, and the next there's fever and sweat and hallucination. After a few such agonies, which no one avoids for long, human flesh begins to live in tense expectation of the next, sure that it will come even if uncertain about the form it will take.

Death is also everywhere, the constant horizon of fragility, the goal toward which fleshly fragility tends. Infants see and touch, uncomprehendingly, dead things, things that were once flesh and are now corpses. Their meaning has to be learned; it is difficult to understand, and difficult to credit when understood. How can it be that this ant, just now moving so fast and purposely (it seems) across the garden path, is now spatchcocked and still? Won't it move again? Why not? Or the rose bloom in the vase, its petals now browning and falling? Why won't it stay as it was, perfect in its blood-red beauty? Most surprising and most difficult: What does it mean that my father (my friend, my mother, my sister) lies waxy still there in the coffin, or crushed and bloody there on the road, or cold and motionless there on the sofa? Why am I being told that I'll never see him move or speak again?

Children do not easily understand or believe what they are told about death, which is because it makes no clear or obvious sense; and even when they do assent to the fact of it, they have no lively sense of its relevance to or inevitability for themselves. They can't imagine the world without themselves in it, and so can't have any real apprehension of their own death. That apprehension comes, however, soon enough, as the flesh decays and as the death of others is seen and understood and leaves its impression. By the fourth or fifth decade of life, if it lasts so long, most human flesh has a deep sense of its own mortality as supplement to, frame for, and inevitable concomitant of its sense of its fragility. It becomes clear that flesh is mortal as well as fragile: that all flesh is grass. Once that is clear, the sense of flesh as not just fragile but mortally so is incised upon it as a scar to be fingered daily.

Pascal, in the *Pensées*, puts the matter like this, when reasoning about the human condition according to natural lights. We all, he writes, see

> un nombre d'hommes dans les chaînes, et tous condamnés à la mort, dont les uns étant chaque jour égorgés à la vue des autres, ceux qui restent voient leur propre condition dans celle de leurs semblables, et, se regardant l'un l'autre avec douleur et sans espérance, attendent à leur tour.

The world is a prison house in which all that's clear is that everyone in it is condemned to death. Daily the prisoners see some of their fellows taken out to be killed; the rest—all of us—hopelessly and sadly wait our turn, knowing that it will come, but neither when nor why. It's hard to disagree.

2   FLESH TRANSFIGURED

JESUS CHRIST, the anointed one of Israel, bears both a name (Jesus) and a title (Christ), and this combination shows what to call him and who he is. According to Christian understanding, he is a double-natured person, at once fully human and fully the LORD. He was and is unique in this, and puzzlingly so, because persons are, ordinarily and by conventional definition, single-natured: they are either human, or divine (Father, Son, Spirit), or, if there are any such persons, simian or fishy or extraterrestrial. The idea of a single person with more than one nature, belonging, therefore, to more than one kind, is opaque at first blush, and perhaps also on last acquaintance. That, however, is what Christian doctrine claims Jesus to be.

This view of Jesus entails that his flesh is human flesh. The triune LORD is fleshless, except for the fact of the incarnation, and so even the flesh of Jesus is not simply the LORD's flesh, but, rather, human flesh transfigured by the fact that it's the flesh of a double-natured person, a divine-human person. That view is essential to the meaning, both conceptual and etymological, of "incarnation," and since the enfleshedness of the Word, the second person of the Trinity, is a central and nonnegotiable item of Christian doctrine, affirming the humanity of Jesus's flesh has the same status. His flesh belongs to his human nature, which is to say that it is human flesh, not divine flesh (there is no such thing), and certainly not flesh of any other kind. It's the human flesh of a divine-human person.

A speculative position in trinitarian theology is that the flesh of Jesus is an atemporal fact about the LORD, and therefore belongs to the trinitarian economy essentially. Slightly more technically, in the metronomic temporal order, according to which time passes and is measurable by clocks and calendars, there was a time before the incarnation, and, therefore, a time when the second person of the Trinity was not enfleshed. But the triune LORD is not subject to that temporal order—the metronome, time whose law is measure, is time damaged, and the LORD is in no way subject to or responsible for damage—and so in the LORD's time, the time of the diastolic/systolic circum-incession of the three persons, what the LORD does in the world, *ad extra*, is atemporally, which is roughly to say, in the language of the metronome, always, present to the LORD. This entails that the flesh of Jesus is always present to the LORD as the flesh of that divine-human person. Which is in turn to say that the *logos asarkos*, the fleshless Word, is a metronomic thought experiment without purchase on the trinitarian economy. There may be reasons for using the locution, but there are none that require Christians to think that it labels anything. (Divisions of Christian opinion about this matter are, without exception, traceable to disagreements about the nature of time.)

Being a person who is both the LORD and human means that Jesus's flesh, though human and thus like ours, is not in every way like ours. Ours is human flesh as found among human creatures whose personhood can be exhaustively understood by appeal to their humanity; his is human flesh proper to a person who is both human and the LORD, both Jesus of Nazareth, born to Mary, and the Christ, the Messiah who is the son of the living god. Ours is human flesh, corrupted by our own sin and damaged by the devastated world into which it is conceived and born; his, like ours, is born into a devastated world and therefore responsive to and affected by the violence and death and damage that characterize such a world, though without the deepening of that damage produced by further sin of his own. Jesus's flesh shows, therefore, both differences from and similarities to our own. Some of the differences are because his flesh belongs to a sinless person; others are due to the transfigurative effects on human flesh of union with the LORD, which is to say that they're due to the fact that the anointed one is a double-natured person. The similarities between his flesh and ours are those that belong to human flesh as such, those without which flesh could not be human.

Jesus's natal flesh (2.1) begins, according to the metronome, in Mary's womb and ends on the cross; it finds itself in a devastated world and accepts the fleshly damage concomitant with being in that world (2.2); it also shows, by transfiguration (2.3), whose flesh it is. After its death on the cross, Jesus's

natal flesh becomes for a short while resurrected flesh (2.4), and this in turn
becomes ascended flesh (2.5), the significant absence around which the life of
the Church is ordered here below.

2.1   Jesus's Natal Flesh

Jesus's flesh, according to scriptural narrative and Christian doctrine, was present in the metronomically timed and spatially gridded world for a span beginning with his conception in Mary's womb and ending with his ascension
some days after the first Easter. That's some thirty years during the early Roman
Empire, probably spanning the imperial reigns of Augustus (27 BC–AD 14) and
Tiberius (AD 14–37). No more exact beginning and ending dates are recover-
able. Jesus's flesh, like all flesh, was placed in space as well as in time (the one
kind of placement entails the other), and that, for him, was a span of a few hundred miles at most, from the Galilee in the north of what is now Israel to parts
of the Sinai Peninsula in what is now Egypt—and mostly in the much narrower
reach between the Galilee and the environs of Jerusalem. It was a short lifespan,
and a geographically constrained one. It's here, metronomically speaking, that
his natal flesh—the flesh of his conception and birth—is found.

These timespace measures place Jesus's flesh according to the metronome
and the grid; all human flesh is placed in these ways. But according to Christian doctrine and practice Jesus's flesh is also, because of his divinity, beyond
the metronome and the grid in a variety of ways. First, that flesh, during its
span of unmediated availability in the devastation, had powers and capacities
not ordinarily proper to human flesh: among other things, it walked on water,
healed the sick, raised the dead, spoke with authority, and was transfigured.
And then, after dying, it was resurrected; a short time later it ascended directly
into heaven; it is, since the ascension, fully available in the form of consecrated
bread and wine to those baptized into his flesh in many places simultaneously,
an availability that has continued for more than two millennia; and it is present
in heaven. Some among these powers and capacities are possible for ordinary
human flesh, too: it may be given to some to heal the sick, to walk on water,
and even to raise the dead with Christ's help, as it was given to some among the
followers of his natal flesh, for example to Peter; Christians will be resurrected,
they hope, eventually; and if so, their risen flesh will, like his, continue to be,
without end and without subjection to the metronome. Even fleshly transfigu-

ration may be possible for some, with Christ's help, as the scriptural account suggests that it was for Moses and Elijah. But all these things, should human flesh be given them, are gifts of participation in the flesh of Jesus; they are possible for human flesh only in that secondary sense, whereas for Jesus they were possible immediately, because he was the LORD as well as a man. And at least one among the capacities of Christ's flesh, that of eucharistic presence, is impossible for human flesh even in these derived and participatory senses.

Jesus's flesh shares in and shows all the ordinary features of human flesh. It's fragile and mortal; it touches and is touched by other flesh, human and otherwise, and is thus constituted properly as flesh; it's placed in the world by its contacts with inanimate bodies; it leaks into the world by way of sweat, blood, spittle, and tears, about which Scripture is explicit, and, by implication, by way of urine, shit, and, perhaps, semen, about which Scripture has nothing to say; it ingests the world, taking in air by breathing, food by eating, and liquid by drinking; it is sexed, as male; it undergoes change and growth, from its conception in Mary's womb to its maturity; and so on. In Jesus's flesh in all these respects, human flesh shows itself with a clarity and ecstasy otherwise unavailable.

Attention to the flesh of Jesus as human flesh involves looking at its similarities to and differences from paradisial flesh, resurrected flesh, and devastated flesh. Two of these comparanda—paradisial flesh (that of Adam and Eve before the fall) and resurrected flesh (that of human creatures raised after their deaths)—aren't directly available. There are, now, since the departure from the garden, no undevastated human creatures and there is therefore no undevastated human flesh. Even Jesus's flesh between conception and ascension was responsive to the damage, including suffering and death, effected by the fall; and Mary's flesh, though perhaps exempt from death because of her immaculacy (a position preferable to its contradictory, though neither required nor ruled out by the dogmatic definition of her assumption into heaven), was subject to suffering and pain. Even their flesh does not provide exceptions to the unavailability of paradisial flesh. Speculative thought is the only device available for understanding that kind of flesh. Similarly, there are now, apart from the ascended flesh of Christ and the assumed flesh of Mary (perhaps also the flesh of Enoch and Elijah, the two individuals of whom Scripture seems to say that they ascended to heaven without dying), no instances of resurrected flesh. All other human flesh is either living now, devastated by the fall's damage; or it has died and ceased thereby to be flesh by returning to body as corpse. Eventually, when the general resurrection has happened, there will be resurrected human (and perhaps also nonhuman) flesh, but at the moment there is not. Differentiating Jesus's flesh—whether as it was from conception to ascension, or as it is after ascension—from paradisial or resurrected flesh is therefore difficult and speculative. Less speculative and less difficult—though still not easy, and still to some extent speculative—is considering Jesus's flesh by comparison to and differentiation from devastated flesh, of which there's plenty. Thinking about Jesus's flesh involves thinking about human flesh, and thinking about human flesh involves thinking about Jesus's flesh, even if that fact isn't always evident to those who think about human flesh.

Jesus's flesh was, according to the time of the metronome, first constituted in Mary's womb and by her womb-caress. The affirmation of fleshly conception and birth is strong and clear in the scriptural nativity stories, and it's been evident since almost the beginning of Christianity that those who aren't comfortable with the idea that Jesus was fleshly and that the flesh in question was human flesh are likely also to be uneasy about, and therefore to downplay the significance of, exactly those stories. Clarity about Jesus's fleshliness brings ease with the nativity stories, which are fleshly from beginning to end. If Jesus was fleshly, then the nativity stories make sense. If not, they don't, and are an embarrassment.

Matthew's Gospel begins with a *liber generationis Iesu Christi*, a book, or account, of the generation, or lineage, of Jesus. It begins with Abraham and traces forty-one generations from him to Joseph, Mary's husband, "from whom"— that is, from Mary—"Jesus was born" as the forty-second generation after Abraham. Luke's genealogy comes later in the story, placed in the third chapter, at the beginning of his account of the work of Christ as adult, and it is more ambitious than Matthew's, tracing, backwards, seventy-five generations from Joseph, Jesus's father *ut putabatur*, "as was supposed," to "Adam, son of God."

Both genealogies show Jesus's Jewishness by placing Abraham in the lineage; Luke, by extending the genealogy to Adam, depicts Jesus as the second Adam. Both, he writes, are sons of God because (he doesn't write, but the reader infers) they lack a human father. This is among the earliest depictions of Jesus as the second Adam, and it's a homology of fleshly origination, of natality. Jesus has a human mother while Adam does not: Adam is created directly by the LORD without any human participation, male or female, while Jesus's conception is *de Spiritu Sancto*, as Matthew has it, or, as Luke puts it more expansively, by means of the Holy Spirit supervening or coming upon Mary, or by the *virtus altissimi*, the power of the Most High, overshadowing her. These tropes are of descent and embrace; they don't provide physiological clues, any more than does the Genesis account of how Adam and Eve were made and quickened. They focus instead on the LORD as the agent who will bring about conception in Mary if she consents to the offer; her agency is essential. Further, Luke's genealogy is given directly after his account of Jesus's baptism. That account ends with the Holy Spirit descending upon Jesus like a dove, and a heavenly voice identifying Jesus as the Father's Son.

The genealogy can be read as an extended gloss on what it means to be son of god, a gloss to which two points are essential. The first is that being son of god means coming to be without a human father; that's the point of the similarity with Adam. Both he and Jesus are sons of the LORD in that sense. The second is that being son of god after the fall, in a world in which human flesh is brought into being always and necessarily in just one way, which is by conception in a woman's womb, or at least by fertilization of a woman's egg, requires a human mother and, therefore, a lineage. Without those things there's no postlapsarian human flesh. That's why Jesus must have a lineage, and it's among the reasons why those among the evangelists who provide accounts of the nativity also give his genealogy.

Both genealogies, too, are particular: they don't simply say that Jesus had a lineage; they show, with names, what it was. The names aren't the same in the two lineages, and the particulars can't be reconciled without spectacular ingenuity. That work is unimportant. What is important is not the names given in the lineages, many of which are mentioned in Scripture nowhere but here, but that there are names—it matters who Jesus's ancestors were, just as it matters for each of us; it's proper to having human flesh that there are ancestors—and that they are Jewish names. Abraham is there in both genealogies. Jesus's flesh is, therefore, Jewish flesh, and his circumcision on the eighth day after his birth writes that fact on his flesh.

Jewish flesh is beloved by, intimate with, and covenanted to the LORD. The same is true of no other human flesh. That's what the election of the Jews comes to, at least as Christian theology understands it. The scriptural emphasis on the Jewishness of Jesus's flesh shows these facts about it to hearers of Scripture. Christians should not be able to avoid understanding and meditating upon Jesus's natal flesh—the flesh conceived, born, and killed in the devastation—as Jewish, covenanted and circumcised to mark these facts. When, at Jesus's baptism, the LORD's voice announces Jesus as the beloved son, among the reasons for his belovedness is that his flesh is Jewish. That is at least a necessary condition for his sonship: a non-Jewish son of the LORD after Abraham's call is a contradiction. It is not, however, a sufficient condition. Being the LORD's son in the flesh requires, in addition to being conceived as a male Jew, which is to say in the womb of a Jewish woman, that the woman's egg be fertilized in the absence of male sperm. When both these things happen—and they have done so only once, as Christians see things—the man so conceived is the LORD's son. A later and more conceptually developed Christian understanding of this deploys the categories of trinitarian doctrine: the LORD's son—a male Jew conceived without a human father—is a double-natured divine-human person, whose divine nature is the second person of the *sanctissima trinitas*, and whose mother is *mater dei*, the LORD's mother. His flesh, therefore, is the human flesh of that person. Such an understanding is at best implicit in the Gospel accounts of Jesus's genealogy and birth; it does, however, provide an interpretation of them fully consistent with what is explicit in them.

The significance of the genealogical establishment of the Jewishness of Jesus's flesh can be underscored in another way. Jesus's flesh is like Adam's, Luke's genealogy shows us, in having come to be without a human father. But Adam's is not Jewish flesh because there are as yet no Jews—Abraham is the first. Adam, although the LORD's son in one sense (the LORD was his only father), wasn't and couldn't be the LORD's son in the sense that Jesus was and is, and that's because he wasn't, and couldn't have been, Jewish. Jewishness, the fact of the people of Israel, chosen by and irrevocably covenanted to the LORD, was a response to and therefore an artifact of the fall. Had there been no fall there would have been no call of Abraham and therefore no Jews. Only when there are Jews—when that means of remedying the fall's damage has been put in place—is Jesus possible. Only then is a divine-human person with Jewish flesh possible. The genealogical display of Jesus's flesh as Jewish writes the incarnation into the covenant and makes the eucharistic flesh that Christians eat a nonnegotiably Jewish presence in the fabric of Christian liturgical life. It's easy to forget this. Christians often have and often do. But such forgetfulness is damaging to Christianity because it makes the Gospel homeless and Jesus's flesh a phantasm, and because it is deeply implicated with Christian violence against the flesh of actual, living Jews.

Suppose the LORD had taken flesh in the womb of a Brahmanical Hindu woman somewhere in the Gangetic plain during the time of Ashoka. Suppose, further, that the LORD so enfleshed was a double-natured divine-human person, who grew, taught, healed, was killed, resurrected, and ascended. Suppose, yet further, that after his ascension his disciples received the gift of the Spirit and began to witness to the triune LORD and to celebrate a eucharist at which they received the ascended LORD's body and blood—which is to say, suppose that they constituted a (or the) church. None of this is prima facie impossible. But it has implications unacceptable to Christian theology. First among these is that the LORD's history with the Jewish people would be extrinsic and incidental to the economy of salvation. Such a church would have no need of the literary record of the LORD's intimacy with the Jews, and would therefore be in every way Marcionite. It would lack an essential property of the Church, which is exactly to be formed by that record as revelation, as *verbum Domini*. The existence of such a church would also mean that the LORD's work of healing the devastated world would either now run along two parallel tracks—a Jewish and an ecclesial one—or, more drastically, that the covenantal intimacy between the LORD and the Jews would be abrogated because there would be a church to which it was irrelevant. This thought experiment shows at least that the idea of a non-Jewish incarnation of the LORD lacks *convenientia*, which is to say the beauty of appropriateness. It may do more. It may show that a non-Jewish incarnation requires the abandonment of the idea of the election of the Jews because it's an idea that only makes sense in a world in which there are no Jews. Once Abraham had been called, the LORD's incarnation could happen only within the context of that calling. Jesus's human flesh had to be Jewish.

The Gospel depictions of the conception and birth of Jesus are deeply fleshly but not grossly physiological. There is no representation of the changes in Mary's body due to pregnancy—the cessation of her periods, the swelling of her belly and breasts, her likely vomiting in the first trimester, the increase in frequency of her urination, the changes in her appetites for food and drink. All these are unmentioned. The same is true of the birth itself: there's no mention of the breaking of Mary's waters, the contractions of her uterus, the pressure on Jesus's body and head as it entered the birth canal, the blood and other bodily fluids that accompanied his birth, the cutting and tying of the umbilicus, the expulsion of the placenta and its disposal, Jesus's first cries and urinations and defecations, his mouth latching on to Mary's breasts and sucking the colostrum therefrom. These, as well as being unmentioned in Scripture, are mostly also undepicted in the later tradition. Christians may, however, acknowledge and delight in them. The conception and birth of Jesus's flesh was the conception and birth of human flesh; it happened, therefore, physiologically speaking, and with the sole exception of Mary's egg's fertilization in the absence of sperm, in just the way that such things happen for humans in the devastated postlapsarian world. The physiological process would have been what it always is; it's a requirement of Christian doctrine to say so; and this is the sense in which Jesus's flesh (and Mary's) can and should be said to have been located in and responsive to the damage done to flesh by the fall's devastation. She, in accord with the curse placed upon Eve, suffers the pains of childbirth; he, in accord with the demands of that curse, is born into the world in a flood of blood and water and mucus and agony, as all babies are—and as is peculiarly appropriate for one from whose side blood and water issue after his death on the cross. Christian devotional practice could easily expand to include meditation on the gross physiological facts of his birth; there would be nothing theologically dubious or unseemly in this, and a good deal to be gained—not least that Jesus's flesh's intimacy with and likeness to ours might be more evident to Christians than it sometimes is.

Jesus often touches the flesh of others and is touched by it between his conception and his ascension. This touch is most intimate and embracing when he's in Mary's womb. Then, as with each of us, his flesh in its entirety is caressed by hers, and can live as flesh only because that's so. Between birth and death, the Gospels mention Jesus being touched by and touching the flesh of others at least twenty times. He is circumcised, baptized, hugged by Simeon, has his feet anointed by Mary of Bethany and wiped with her hair, is bound and whipped and crucified, is kissed, washes the feet of others, caresses children, and heals the flesh of others by touching it. The Gospels don't provide a full account of Jesus's fleshly exchanges, but what they do give us shows almost no embarrassment about these fleshly exchanges. His flesh, like ours, was constituted as flesh by frequent caresses exchanged with his mother, father (as was supposed), friends, and acquaintances; he used touch, as we do, as a means of healing and comfort; and he was subject in the flesh to wounding, inflicted by the violent touches of others. He, like us, received his flesh as flesh by touch from the flesh of others.

2.2 Jesus's Damaged Flesh

Jesus was killed by violence, and before his crucifixion was whipped and otherwise tortured. While the Gospels don't show much interest in the details of these tortures, or in the particulars of Jesus's fleshly response to them, they say enough to make clear the fragility of his flesh when treated violently or threatened with violence, and its ordinary responses to whipping and wounding. Those responses include bleeding when wounded, and dying when tortured beyond endurance. This kind of fragility is proper to human flesh in a chaotically violent world (1.5); it is what belongs to the flesh, and Jesus's flesh exhibits it as ours does. Jesus's flesh is wounded; but there is no scriptural instance of, nor any traditional emphasis upon, Jesus's flesh inflicting wounds on the flesh of others. He is wounded, but does not wound.

It is clear, abundantly so, that Scripture represents Jesus's flesh as capable of sustaining damage by human action, including action that uses weapons or other instruments of violence. It's also clear that Jesus is represented in Scripture as responding to events as if he knows this to be the case: he runs, sometimes, when it seems that others are planning to capture or wound him, which implies that he judges it possible for them to do these things should he permit them to—as, eventually, he does, with the arrest in Gethsemane. But it is much less clear that Jesus's flesh can be damaged by occurrences that don't involve human agency. Such might include: illness produced by nonhuman agents (bacteria, viruses) acting from without on his flesh; fleshly damage effected by the violence of the inanimate world (fire, flood); damage brought about by the decay of the flesh without the action of external agents (loss of hair, of muscle tone, of eyesight). About the first and third of these, Scripture has nothing to say one way or the other. Jesus is there depicted neither as subject to nor immune from illness; the same is true of the fleshly effects of aging—though in that case it is suggestive that Scripture depicts Jesus as dying before he was of an age (according to the norms of the time; our norms are different) to show any such effects, and the later tradition has made a good deal of this point. But about the second of these, fleshly damage produced by the violence of the inanimate world, there are some suggestive scriptural passages.

Luke, for example, in his eighth chapter, shows Jesus in a boat on a stormy lake. Others in the boat are frightened; they can see that the waves might sink their boat and drown them—*perimus*, they say—we're dying. Jesus, however, is asleep, and when the others wake him, he tells the wind and water to be calm, and at once they are. He then says to his followers, *ubi est fides vestra?*, implying that if they'd only had faith they wouldn't have worried. They'd have been like him in this respect: certain that the water couldn't harm them. Those in the boat are astonished, saying to one another, *quis putas hic est, quia et ventris imperat et aqua, et oboediunt ei?*—who do you think this is, who commands wind and water and gets obedience? Among the points made by the story is the thought that the flesh of Jesus is immune to damage caused by nonhuman (and in this case inanimate) agents unless he permits it. These things are under his control. He is their *imperator* because he is the LORD, and they must hear him and do what he says. The text suggests that Jesus's flesh is not subject to damage against his will from nonhuman agents; and, further, that he doesn't in fact permit such damage to occur. Scripture, at any rate, records no instances. This clearly differentiates fleshly damage caused by nonhuman agents from that caused by humans. Scripture records many instances of Jesus permitting the latter, and none of the former.

Consider also the scriptural story of the temptations in the desert, given, with different details and structure, in the fourth chapters of Matthew's and of Luke's Gospels. This episode involves a forty-day abstention from at least food and possibly also water. Matthew's expression, *et cum ieiunasset quadraginta diebus*—and when he had fasted forty days—implies, ordinarily, neither food nor water; Luke's *nihil manducavit*—he ate nothing—is more naturally read to indicate abstention only from things chewed or masticated, and thus from solid food only. At the end of that time, both Matthew and Luke write that he was hungry (*esuriit*). The point of the story is not to consider whether Jesus would have died if he'd fasted, whether from food or liquid or both, for longer than forty days (though it's worth noting that it is unlikely that anyone could survive a forty-day desert sojourn without water). The point is rather to show that he suffered in the flesh because of the fast. This might seem to suggest that Jesus was in his natal flesh subject to the ordinary demands of the flesh for food and drink. If not, why would he have been hungry? But in fact, matters are not so clear, even in this case. Jesus was, when he went out into the wilderness, *plenus Spiritu Sancto*, which is at least to say that he performs this fast and embraces its effects deliberately and for a purpose. That purpose is to show that he is not subject to *Diabolus/Satanas*; he fasts exactly in order that he might, while hungry, reject the idea that he should, as the adversary suggests, turn the stones of the desert into bread. Had he been subject to hunger as we are—about to die from it, as we would be—he would have made the stones into bread and eaten them. That he doesn't suggests that he bears the same relation to the ordinary effects of lack of food upon human flesh as he does to the ordinary effects of stormy seas upon human flesh. That is a relation of authority. Those things can damage his natal flesh only to the extent that he permits; and this in turn means that the double-natured person didn't need to eat as we do. He ate, certainly, in his natal flesh and after; but not doing so would not have killed him, and doing so served a particular, providential purpose.

A similar line can be taken about the other two categories of fleshly damage: those produced by illness and by aging. About those too it can be said that Jesus's natal flesh wasn't subject to them in the sense that they had no power over him. He would have permitted them power (and in permitting it to them would have shown it precisely not to be power but rather a gift granted them) only to the extent that it served some providential purpose to do so, as in the case of the hunger produced by fasting in the desert, or in the case of the damage done to his flesh by the whip and the thorns and the nails. The rubric under which all these cases can be placed is Jesus's denial of coercive power to Pilate at his trial as recounted by John: *non haberes potestatem adversum me ullam, nisi tibi esset datum desuper*—you'd have no power at all over me, unless it had been given you from above. Just as it seemed to Pilate that he had the power to have Jesus crucified no matter what Jesus thought about it, so the invasive virus or decaying cell might seem to have power to damage Jesus's flesh. But in none of these cases was it so. Whatever power they had was granted them by the LORD, and always for providential purposes, which means that in some cases it was granted and in others not. In no case is the LORD, here the double-natured person Jesus Christ, subject to them simply because of what they are and what he is. Devastated human flesh, by contrast, is subject to these inflictors of fleshly damage exactly for that reason: the virus kills us, the sword cuts us, and our muscles wither and our bones weaken by necessities independent of our intentions and radically excessive to any power we can muster over them. Our flesh, devastated by the fall, simply is subject to these necessities. Jesus's flesh was not.

—But isn't this docetism, a view long rejected by the Church and not capable of accommodation into orthodox Christianity? Doesn't this way of putting things amount to the claim that there was no real taking of flesh by the LORD? That his apparent flesh-taking was just that—apparent, not real? Doesn't the position make of Jesus, the incarnate one, a kind of Superman walking among us, his flesh invulnerable to the slings and arrows of ordinary fleshly damage unless he chooses to make it otherwise?

—No. It isn't docetism. Jesus, according to the view just set down, really is enfleshed; his flesh really is fleshly, really is human flesh, conceived in a woman's womb and born in the ordinary way. But it's human flesh undamaged by sin in any of its forms, whether actively committed by Jesus, which is an impossibility according to the grammar of orthodox Christian speech, or inherited by him as damage passed on by his parents and ancestors, which is also an impossibility within the grammar of orthodox Catholicism, even if not so clearly for that of non-Catholic Christianity. If death and its servants—illness and aging—are effects of the fall, brought about, therefore, exactly as damage to something—flesh—to which they are properly extrinsic, then the fact that Jesus's flesh is exempt from them doesn't show it not to be flesh. It shows, rather, that his flesh is human flesh undamaged, like (in this respect, though not in all others) Eve's and Adam's, and like ours as it will be after the resurrection. The view, therefore, isn't docetism; it's exactly and properly incarnational, exactly and properly what it would be for the LORD to take flesh. But yes, the view entertained here does amount to the assertion of Jesus's invulnerability. He cannot be damaged in the flesh unless he assents to that damage, and he is in this respect deeply unlike us. That shouldn't trouble Christians. We already know—Christian orthodoxy requires—that his flesh came to be without a woman's egg being fertilized by a man's sperm; we already know—Christian orthodoxy requires—that his flesh became a corpse on the cross, and then, roughy thirty-six hours later, became flesh again, and then, forty or so days after that, ascended. None of this is possible for our flesh as presently constituted. After this camel, to strain at the gnat of Jesus's invulnerability to the ordinary damage of the devastation is unnecessary. So, the speculative position about Jesus's invulnerability in his natal flesh survives both the objection that it's docetic, and the objection that it makes him into an implausible and perhaps repellent Superman.

There is, however, another possible view about the vulnerability of Jesus's flesh, perhaps best thought of as a variant of the view just defended. It's the view that Jesus's providential permission for damage to his flesh isn't occasional, as Scripture's depiction suggests, but rather generic. That is, it isn't that Jesus gives case-by-case providential permission—permission for damage by this fast, that whip, those nails—but rather that the consent to incarnation carried with it permission for any and all such things to damage Jesus's flesh, just as they would any human flesh, *post lapsum*. Such a permission, were it to have belonged to the incarnation, would have meant that Jesus's flesh would have been damaged from time to time by viruses, falls, fights, and so on, as human flesh ordinarily is. This view makes Jesus's flesh less like Superman's, and more like ours; this also makes it easier, perhaps, for latter-day Christians to identify with Jesus and to understand their own quotidian fleshly sufferings as imitative of and participatory in his. These are advantages for the view just to the extent that these things are taken to be of importance for the Christian life. It's a disadvantage for the view that it sits much less well with Scripture than does the occasionalist position.

Both views, however, are possible, because each is compatible with the formalities of the Christian position on Jesus's natal flesh, which are: said flesh is fully human flesh; it is not subject to sin-wrought damage except when the LORD gives providential permission that it should be; and it shows what undamaged—properly and fully functioning—human flesh is like, also showing, therefore, what human flesh will be like when (if) resurrected for eternal life, and something of what Eve's and Adam's flesh was like before the Fall. Any position on the damage undergone by Jesus's flesh that abides by these constraints is a defensibly Christian one. Those inclined to the view that Jesus's natal flesh was generally vulnerable to ordinary damage and only occasionally exempt from it will think that providential purposes are served by this state of affairs, and will encourage Christians to meditate upon Jesus's fleshly vulnerability. Those inclined to the view of his general invulnerability with occasional providential exceptions will think that Jesus's natal flesh shows important things about what ordinary human resurrected flesh will be like, and will encourage Christians to think on those. These are differences of emphasis, not differences of contradiction.

Whichever view about the vulnerability of Jesus's natal flesh turns out to be true, the constraints upon what can count as a Christian view on the matter are now clear. No member of this family of speculative views is, or needs to be, also a view about Jesus's subjectivity. That is a separate question, and not one of any significance to Christian theology. Consider, for instance, how attention to that question can distort the account of Jesus's stilling of the storm: Jesus, having been asleep in a boat on a stormy sea, is woken by his frightened companions, and says (in Matthew's version of the story), *Quid timidi estis, modico fidei?*—What are you frightened of, you with hardly any faith? Then, he rebukes the wind and waves—the text doesn't show how—and everything becomes quiet. Should hearers of the text speculate about how these events seemed to Jesus—about what it seemed like to him to be in this situation, to say and do these things? Scripture, as is typical, shows no interest in this, which is to say no interest in Jesus's subjectivity, in the phenomenal properties of his experience, in what it seemed like to him to be a storm-stiller. To think such matters important, and to attend to them, is to miss the point of the story, which is to show something about Jesus's relation to storms and about the importance of having faith in a person with that relation. Even in cases of direct and effective fleshly touch—Jesus's flesh is whipped, pressed upon by the flesh of others, touched in such a way as to effect a healing—or in cases where Jesus acts in such a way as to suggest to most hearers that he's suffering—he groans or weeps—Scripture is chaste in the extreme about depicting or commenting upon what it seems like to Jesus to be Jesus. The question of the flesh, by contrast—what it is like, what it can do, what its vulnerabilities and purposes are—is directly relevant to the Christian life, of deep theological interest, and central to scriptural portrayals of Jesus.

Scripture sometimes represents the vulnerability of Jesus's natal flesh; when it does, it also provides context or explanation that makes the providential purpose of the exhibition of such vulnerability clear. Scripture also sometimes represents the invulnerability of Jesus's natal flesh, or at least some property or aspect of that flesh that approaches invulnerability. It does that about as often as it represents vulnerability, and less frequently with context or explanation that makes the providential purpose of those representations evident. This asymmetry suggests that it was obvious enough to the evangelists that Jesus's natal flesh could act in ways not possible for ordinary human natal flesh; that it could do so was the norm—isn't this the Gospel of the Son of God, as Mark writes at the beginning of his Gospel, and wouldn't one expect the natal flesh of such a one to be unusual? Doesn't the weakness and vulnerability of that flesh create more difficulties and prompt more comment than its unusual powers and capacities—powers such as walking on water (fleshly invulnerability to water's contact), healing by the touch of one's garment (not even by direct fleshly contact) without knowing in advance that this was to happen, or having one's flesh radiantly transfigured while in the apparently living company of some who have died long before?

2.3   Jesus's Transfigured Flesh

Matthew's account of the transfiguration, in the seventeenth chapter of his Gospel, has it that Jesus takes Peter and James and John up an unnamed mountain for an unspecified purpose. There, he's "transfigured (*transfiguratus*) before them," which is specified in the Gospel to mean that his face is resplendent like the sun and his clothes dazzlingly white. The verb used for the radiance of his face, *resplendere*, suggests the emission of light from within rather than re-flected light, as does the likening of his face to the sun. Then, Moses and Elijah appear with him, and the three of them talk. The text doesn't say what they talk about, and doesn't describe how Moses and Elijah appear on the scene. It gives an iconic tableau: sharp and still and radiant, appearing suddenly and inexplicably before the faces of Peter, James, and John, as also before the Gospel's hearers. The atmosphere is one of dream or vision, as Peter's first response suggests: *Domine, bonum est nos hic esse*—LORD, it's good for us to be here. He goes on to ask Jesus whether he might make three tabernacle tents (*tabernacula*) to house the radiant bodies of flesh in front of him. But while he's making this suggestion, a radiant cloud (*nubes lucida*) covers them all, and from it a voice speaks, saying, "this is my beloved son in whom I'm well pleased; listen to him." Peter, James, and John are overcome by fear when they hear this, and fall to the ground. Jesus then comes and touches them (*tetigit eos*). Is his face still radiant? The text doesn't say. Does his healing hand share in the radiance of his face? The text doesn't say—and tells them to get up and leave their fear behind. They look up and see only Jesus. Moses and Elijah have gone, and (perhaps) Jesus's flesh no longer shines. They come down from the mountain, and Jesus tells them to keep silent about the vision—now it's explicitly called that—*donec Filius hominis a mortuis resurgat*—until the Son of Man shall rise from the dead.

The account isn't further explained, although it is immediately followed in Matthew by an identification of John the Baptist with Elijah. The account as a whole is full of resonances with other parts of Scripture. Moses's face is described in the thirty-fourth chapter of Exodus as shining (*resplendere*, the same verb used in the Matthean account of the resurrection as well as in that of the transfiguration) when he comes down from the mountain after receiving the tablets of the law, and that's because he's been talking with the LORD. Fleshly radiance on Jesus's part suggests, with this echo in mind, the intimacy of Jesus's natal flesh with the LORD; but his fleshly glow differs from Moses's in that it isn't presented as the result of an encounter with the LORD—it's shown, rather, as self-generated, a feature of his natal flesh. The presence of the cloud in the account of the transfiguration also has Mosaic echoes, both because Moses's encounters with the LORD are often cloud-shrouded in one way or another, and because of the veil Moses uses to shroud the radiance of his face when he's not talking with the LORD. And the voice from the cloud in Matthew's version of the transfiguration repeats, almost verbatim, the words spoken from above at Jesus's baptism—which is another similarity to the Exodus account of Moses's radiant face.

Peter's proposal to house the radiantly transfigured flesh of Jesus in a tabernacle-tent connects the event on the mountain to the Feast of Booths (tents, tabernacles). The Latin word used in the New Vulgate's rendering of Matthew's account of the transfiguration is the same as that text's version of the requirements for the feast, as found, for example, in the twenty-third chapter of Leviticus. This was, and is, a feast required of the Jewish people in remembrance of their wanderings in the wilderness after leaving Egypt. It became also, over time, a feast to which the honored dead (Moses and Elijah, especially) could be invited with some expectation that they might attend, and, in part because of that, a feast at which wilderness commemoration was combined with anticipation of what things might be like when the Messiah had come. All this is in play in the account of Jesus's transfigured natal flesh. It is the Messiah's flesh, which is also the flesh of the LORD; Peter's thought that it might be tabernacled, which isn't rebutted by Jesus in the Matthean account, nor in any other way undercut (as it is in Mark's version of the story), points forward, for Christian hearers, to the ecclesial habit of tabernacling Jesus's ascended eucharistic flesh, and that anticipation closely assimilates Jesus's transfigured natal flesh to the ascended flesh.

The details of the account of the transfiguration—in this case in Matthew, but also in different ways in Mark and Luke—show, suggestively, and with some literary and conceptual elegance, that Jesus's natal flesh can manifest at a single moment what it was (born and baptized), what it is (here now, before the face), and what it will be (risen, ascended, eucharistically edible). Not only that: this natal/risen/ascended/eucharistic flesh touches his terrified followers before they come down from the mountain and therefore, arguably, while it is still transfigured. The touch of Jesus's natal flesh is also the touch of that flesh in all its other states, and this shows that and how it can exhibit the powers and invulnerabilities that it does.

2.4 Jesus's Resurrected Flesh

Jesus's resurrected flesh is the flesh that was intermittently present to various followers between the Sunday after his crucifixion and the time, perhaps forty days later, when he was lifted or carried up (*ferebatur*, in Luke), or elevated (*elevatus*, in Acts), out of their sight in the event that has come to be known as the Ascension, and which is celebrated, liturgically, forty days after Easter Sunday. After that, Jesus's flesh no longer appears to or otherwise interacts with anyone in the form or under the guise of human flesh. Jesus's resurrected flesh therefore has a short life, and is in many ways distinct from both his ascended flesh, which follows it in the metronomic order of time, and from his natal flesh, which precedes it in that order. Jesus's ascended flesh is, in human form, beyond the possibility of haptic interaction with anyone or anything, as it is also beyond the possibility of other modes of sensory interaction; his natal flesh is fully available to the flesh of others exactly as flesh: it often exchanges fleshly touches with others. His ascended flesh is fully available to the baptized in the form of bread. And his resurrected flesh provides an intermediate and ambiguous case.

First, the resurrected flesh is ordinarily unrecognizable as Jesus—more precisely, unrecognizable as Jesus's natal flesh. Those to whom it appears or shows itself typically need a cue additional to the fleshly presence in order to recognize and acknowledge it as the flesh of Jesus. When, as Luke describes in his twenty-fourth chapter, the risen Jesus walks for some miles with two who have (it seems) been acquainted with his natal flesh, and talks with them for some time, they don't recognize him. That happens only when, dining with them, *accepit panem et benedixit ac fregit et porrigebat illis*—he took bread and blessed and broke it and gave it to them, whereupon, *aperti sunt oculi eorum et cognoverunt eum*—their eyes were opened and they knew him. Similarly, in John's description of the risen Jesus's appearance to Mary Magdalene, when she's faced with him, *non sciebat quia Jesus est*—she didn't know it was Jesus. She thinks the person facing her might be the gardener, until he calls her by name, whereupon she does recognize and acknowledge him and tells others as soon as she can that she's seen him. And when, also in John, Jesus is depicted showing (*manifestare*) himself to his followers at the Sea of Tiberias where they're fishing, they have no idea who's talking to them until he tells them where to cast their nets. Only then do they find themselves able to say, *Dominus est.* The unrecognizability of the flesh absent an act of self-communication or self-revelation is at the heart of each of these passages. And even when the resurrected flesh appears to be known as Jesus at once and without difficulty, that is typically because it has appeared suddenly or in an unusual way—in the midst of a gathering behind closed and locked doors, for instance. In these cases too, the simple presence of the resurrected flesh doesn't suffice for recognition; that's produced by the shock of an additional, self-revealing act.

Second, Jesus's resurrected flesh ordinarily doesn't observe the spatiotemporal restrictions placed on human flesh. His natal flesh is sometimes shown in Scripture as not doing so either, as we have seen: it walks on water or mysteriously escapes the attentions of a crowd eager to do it harm. But these cases are exceptions to the rule that the natal flesh does observe the ordinary unities of time and space. The norm is upended in the case of the resurrected flesh. It appears and disappears like a firefly's glow on a summer night, and isn't hindered in its coming and going by material obstructions ordinarily insuperable for human flesh. It's this feature of the resurrected flesh that leads Jesus's followers to ask, in Luke's twenty-fourth chapter, whether he might be discarnate, a *spiritus*. He denies this, emphasizing that he has flesh (*caro*) and bones (*ossa*) as spirits do not. But it's hard not to see the question as a reasonable one. If Jesus's resurrected flesh can disappear and appear at will, and is not ordinarily recognizable to those who've known his natal flesh without some additional revelatory act, why might it not be thought of as something other than flesh?

Jesus's resurrected flesh's liminal and transitional condition is marked by the ambiguity of its fleshly relations with those to whom it appears. Three episodes make clear the oddity of haptic exchange with the resurrected flesh.

First, there's the account in Luke's twenty-fourth chapter of Jesus's self-revelation to the eleven in Jerusalem, together with those who had come to Jerusalem from Emmaus to tell the eleven about Jesus's appearance there.

> As they were speaking about these things, the very one (*ipse*) stood among them and said to them, "Peace be with you." Startled and terrified (*conturbati vero et conterriti*), they thought they were seeing a spirit. He said to them, "What startles you, and why are your hearts full of questions? See my hands and feet: I am the very one (*ipse ego sum*). Touch me and see (*palpate me et videte*): a spirit doesn't have flesh and bones (*carnem et ossa*) as you see I have." When he'd said this, he showed them his hands and feet (*ostendit eis manus et pedes*). While they still didn't believe for joy, and were amazed, he said to them, "Have you something here to eat?" They gave him a piece of broiled fish, and, taking it, he ate it in front of them.

Jesus shows himself here to his followers as the selfsame (*ipse*, twice repeated) in a double sense. He is the one about whom they'd been talking, the one upon whom all expectation and hope and doubt are focused. He is also the same as the one who'd been crucified and laid in the tomb just a few days earlier. And, to extend the resonance of the pronoun *ipsum* only a little, he is the one, selfsame, as the one who is often called *idipsum*, the selfsame, in the Old Testament—for example, in the fourth Psalm—and who is the triune LORD. Jesus shows himself in this triple sense by appearing, suddenly and without explanation, among those who are talking about him. This is another instance of Jesus's resurrected flesh not observing the unities of metronomic timespace. Those gathered don't see him arrive; suddenly, he's there. They're surprised and frightened, and they wonder whether he's a *spiritus*—a being exactly capable of such things because not constrained by the flesh. Jesus responds by showing them the very flesh in question, and commanding them to look (*videte*) at it and touch (*palpate*) it. The text does explicitly say that they look at and see his flesh. It does not say, in spite of his command to do so, that they do touch, or palpate, it. Neither does the text say that they don't. Most hearers of the text, probably, themselves supply the act of touching by assuming that Jesus's followers do what he says they should do. But the text's silence on the question leaves open the possibility that they do not, and that silence underscores the nature of the fleshly availability of Jesus's resurrected flesh, which is that while Jesus can and does show (*ostendere*, usually) his resurrected flesh as flesh to his followers, and can emphasize, as he does in this passage, that what he's showing them exactly is flesh (*caro et ossa*), and can even tell them to touch it, it is not in fact fully available for fleshly interaction. Jesus eats at the conclusion of this Lukan passage, as he also does in John, and there is no textual silence or ambivalence about that. It's by eating that he convinces his followers that he is flesh; touching his flesh is not shown to serve that purpose (the followers are, the text permits us to say, convinced without touching), and if this is a possible reading, Jesus's offer (command) of an exchange of touch with his resurrected flesh is one that can, and possibly should, be refused.

In this line, too, is Thomas the Apostle's encounter with the risen LORD recounted in John's twentieth chapter. Thomas wants to see and to touch Jesus's wounds; if that isn't possible, he won't, he says, believe that Jesus has been resurrected. But when Jesus appears to Thomas eight days later—again ignoring the ordinary unities of time and space, standing among them (exactly the same phrase as in Luke) even though the door is closed—and commands him to do what he'd said he wanted to do, "Place (*infer*) your finger here. . . . Put (*affer*) your hand," Thomas is not shown by the text to do what Jesus commands. What he is shown as doing is making a confession (*Dominus meus et Deus meus*), and that without touching the wounds. Again, the text can be heard to suggest, silently, that Thomas did touch Jesus; but Jesus's concluding words to Thomas use the vocabulary of seeing and looking rather than that of touching ("You've believed because you've seen"), and this supports the reading that interprets the text's silence to mean that Thomas did not touch Jesus. Thomas is not said to believe because he touched. Jesus's command is likely here refused, and that is because conviction that Jesus's resurrected flesh is right here doesn't require touch and might be inhibited by it. The text here is best read to continue the theme of insulating Jesus's risen flesh from touch.

A third and final text along these lines is John's account, in his twentieth chapter, of Jesus's appearance to Mary Magdalene. Mary stands weeping out-side the tomb where she has thought Jesus's dead body might be. When she looks in, she sees two angels and exchanges words with them, explaining that she doesn't know where Jesus's body has been placed, and imploring them to tell her. Then she turns around and *videt Iesum stantem*—sees Jesus inexplica-bly and suddenly standing in front of her. She doesn't recognize him, and takes him to be the gardener (as we saw just above). But then Jesus addresses her by name and she does recognize him. Immediately, without explanation, Jesus says to her, *noli me tenere, nondum enim ascendi ad Patrem*—don't hold on to me; I've not yet ascended to the Father. The implication is that Mary has tried to touch or grab him, in some way to exchange fleshly touch with him; and the reason that Jesus gives for his demand that she not do so contains the only use of the verb *ascendere* in the accounts of the resurrected flesh in the Gos-pels and Acts. The proscription is explicit in marking the ambiguous status of the resurrected flesh in the between-time of the resurrection. Jesus's natal flesh could be touched, and often was; his ascended flesh is touched, intimately, all the time (2.5). But it's because his resurrected flesh has not yet ascended—not yet become available for touch as eucharistic flesh—and because it is no longer limited by the ordinary spacetime unities, as his natal flesh largely was, that it's not to be touched, and especially not to be touched by force, grabbed and held on to, as Mary might have wanted to do. Jesus's resurrected flesh, like his transfigured natal flesh, is dazzlingly dangerous; and attempts to hold on to it, to keep it where it is by placing it in tabernacle tents, or by grasping it, of-fend against its nature. It is on its way somewhere (*ascendo ad Patrem meum et Patrem vestrum, et Deum meum et Deum vestrum*), and until it's arrived there it is unavailable as flesh. Significantly, when Mary returns to the followers to give them the message, she says, *vidi Dominum*, rather than *palpavi Dominum*, both because she hasn't done the latter and because the latter would have been inappropriate or impossible. The resurrected flesh is to be seen and heard, not touched, and for the most part that's what Scripture depicts.

But there is one clear example in Scripture of the resurrected flesh being touched. It's in the twenty-eighth chapter of Matthew's Gospel. Jesus meets the women running from the tomb after they've been told by an angel that he has risen and that they'll see him in Galilee. He greets them, and they fall down (*accesserunt*) before him, grabbing and holding on to his feet as a way of adoring him (*tenuerunt pedes eius et adoraverunt eum*). The women's grasp of Jesus's feet is the same action, indicated by the same verb, *tenere*, that he proscribes for Mary in John's Gospel. Here, he doesn't rebuke the women for grabbing his feet; he simply instructs them to go and tell his followers to go to Galilee where they'll see him (*ibi me videbunt*). The episode, read alone, suggests little about the relation between touching and seeing the resurrected flesh; read in the context of the other accounts of the resurrected flesh, it stands as an anomaly. Jesus's resurrected flesh is here taken by force, it may be, rather than simply touched. That reading is supported by the use of the same verb to indicate what the women do to Jesus's resurrected flesh as was used to indicate what Mary is told not to do. There's a rebuke implicit in that lexical fact.

The resurrected flesh is veiled: the ordinary cues that permit visual recognition aren't there, and this veiling goes with a ban on touch. Neither visual nor tactile intimacy with it are possible for those few with whom it has to do, unless an additional invitation is proffered by Jesus—an invitation that either involves a return to the natal flesh, as when the risen LORD addresses Mary Magdalene by name, or an anticipation of the ordinary mode of tactile availability of the ascended flesh, as when bread is broken and distributed after the walk on the Emmaus road. These unveilings temporarily remove the inaccessibility of Jesus's resurrected flesh to the senses, and they are of short duration and with deep reservation. Even when the resurrected LORD is seen and known, he isn't to be touched: the act of recognition, which he makes possible, points always away from what is recognized—the resurrected flesh—and toward something else as yet not present. The resurrected flesh is there to show that it is superfluous, except to indicate its own superfluity as anything other than a preparation for what is to come, which is the availability of the ascended flesh to the community of followers.

There's a structural parallel here with the eucharistic rite, as also with the order of the three days of Easter. The natal flesh, born to Mary and present in the world, is limited, in its availability, to the small spatiotemporal area of its work, and that work is, mostly, subject to the ordinary spatiotemporal unities. In order to become universally available, the natal flesh needs to be consecrated exactly for such availability, and this is done by its death on Friday. When the natal flesh becomes resurrected flesh, on Sunday, it has been consecrated, and, in terms of the eucharistic rite, this is when the celebrant, having said the words of institution, raises the host—now the flesh of Jesus—before the faces of the Christian people and says, "the gifts of God for the people of God." That is the resurrected flesh. Still, however, at this stage the flesh is available only visually: it can be seen, and recognized (as with the resurrection appearances in Galilee and Jerusalem) under the veil (in the one case a veil of bread, and in the other of flesh that requires self-revelation for recognition), but it can't yet be touched. In the case of the eucharist, touch—the breadflesh and wineblood on the tongue in a touch which is also a taste—doesn't happen until those who seek it have confessed their unworthiness to receive it (*non sum dignus . . .*). Then, and only then, are they asked forward to touch the flesh of Christ—and not now the risen flesh of Christ, but, rather, the ascended flesh of Christ, whose principal mode of availability is under the veil of bread and wine in the eucharist. Just as the eucharistic/ascended flesh can't be touched (tasted) at once, and is no longer looked at as the followers avert their gaze when they fall to their knees (*viri Galilaei, quid statis aspicientes in caelum?*—men of Galilee, why do you stand looking up to heaven? the angels ask the assembled faithful in Jerusalem after Jesus has ascended in the first chapter of Acts) to confess their unworthiness, so also the resurrected flesh vanishes from the gaze, having already been barred from the touch by ascending. Once ascended, it is again touchable, and in the most intimate way, by the tongue.

2.5 Jesus's Ascended Flesh

Two affirmations are required of Christians about Jesus's ascended flesh. The first is that the ascended flesh is at the right hand of the Father, which is a frequent scriptural and creedal affirmation; and the second is that the ascended flesh, together with its blood, are fully and really present, though in a veiled way, in the eucharist. These affirmations suggest, at first blush, a double mode of presence. The first is eschatological. Jesus's ascended flesh is present somewhere and somewhen, in intimate relation to the Father, but inaccessible to humans by touch, and therefore inaccessible as flesh, because they aren't where and when it is. It'll be haptically available, available as flesh, only to human resurrected flesh, which will be before its face. That won't happen until the general resurrection, which is the immediate prelude to the last things proper. That's why Jesus's ascended flesh at the Father's right hand has an eschatological presence only. It cannot be touched now, even if, in dream and vision, it might sometimes be seen. The second mode of the ascended flesh's presence is, by contrast, fully tactile: it's edible; it can be caressed with the tongue and ingested. It's also available for fleshly exchange in many different timespaces at once because it is definitively and completely freed from the unities of metronomic timespace. That is because it occupies the fold of eucharistic time that is identically and at once available to every moment measured by the metronome, and every place located by map grid. The principle mode of tactile availability of the ascended flesh is, then, as the eucharist.

Saul's encounter with Jesus on the road to Damascus is a revealing instance of non-eucharistic encounter with the ascended flesh of Christ. As told in Acts, Saul is approaching Damascus when *subito circumfulsit eum lux*—suddenly a light shone around him. He falls to his knees, and hears himself addressed by name and asked why he's persecuting the speaker. Saul asks who's speaking, but even before hearing the answer he acknowledges the speaker as LORD. *Quis es, Domine?*, he says, asking, exactly as Moses did, for the name of someone he already knows is the LORD. The voice names itself as Jesus, and tells Saul to get up and go into the city where he'll get instructions about what to do next. Those with him, the text says, are astonished, *audientes quidem vocem, neminem autem videntes*—hearing the voice, but seeing no one. The implication isn't necessarily that Saul has seen someone; the text can be read to this point to suggest that he's as surprised as the others to hear a voice without seeing anyone, for all that's been said so far is that he was surrounded by (and, presumably, saw) light. That reading is supported by what's written next in the text, which is that when he opens his eyes he can see nothing. He's blind for the next three days. The text hasn't said that he closed his eyes. Perhaps the suggestion is that he did so in response to the light, which then turns out to have blinded him. There is in any case no hint in the text that Saul sees Jesus's ascended flesh in anything like human form. Later, when Barnabas reports the event to others, he does say that Saul-now-Paul saw the LORD (*in via vidisset Dominum*). The preferable reading of the text as a whole, however—though certainly not the only possible reading—is that there is no vision of the ascended flesh on the Damascus road. Saul sees light and hears the voice of the ascended Jesus; he hears Jesus, but sees only radiance. The light that visually signals Jesus's presence is too radiant for human eyes, and so Saul is blinded—an ordinary response to the approach of the ascended flesh, inseparable as it now is from the Father at whose right hand it is located. The ascended flesh of Christ will be visible to the eyes of the risen flesh, but until then it's visible—even to Saul about to become Paul—only as in a glass, darkly. The trans-local and trans-temporal eucharistic presence of the ascended flesh requires the absence to our senses of the human ascended flesh, and this is a point underscored by the particulars of the scriptural account of the event in which this comes closest to not being so. The veil is not removed, even for Paul.

The eucharistic presence of Jesus's ascended flesh, whether as object of visual adoration in the monstrance or as lingual caress in the eucharist, is the source and summit of the Church's life, and, therefore, the condition of the possibility of all the sacraments, including baptism. If baptism is the sacrament of cleaving, the sacrament whereby human flesh becomes Christian flesh (3.1), then the eucharist is the sacrament of ingestion, whereby already-Christian flesh is nourished and filled with the very flesh to which it has already been cleaved. Baptism precedes eucharist (cleaving precedes eating) in the order of a single Christian life; but eucharist precedes baptism (eating precedes cleaving) in the order of the Church's foundation and, therefore, in the order of being. Once Jesus has been eaten, proleptically at the last supper and at Emmaus, the Church is constituted; and once the Church is constituted, Spirit-filled at Pentecost and Spirit-guided since, cleaving to it becomes possible. And the principal condition of the possibility of the eucharist is exactly that Jesus has ascended. His natal and resurrected flesh can't be eaten, even though that possibility is foreshadowed by what each of them does and says. His resurrected flesh can't even be touched, except by inappropriate force. But after the ascension, his flesh, veiled as bread, and his blood, veiled as wine, can be touched and tasted everywhere and at once, without constraint by the metronome of time or the map grid of space. The Jesus-cleaved can and do adore and receive his ascended flesh simultaneously in Tokyo and Chicago, Kinshasa and Omsk, London and Rome, and even while orbiting the planet Earth.

This is a strange state of affairs. Catholic doctrine requires the simultaneous real presence and availability of Jesus's ascended flesh to the lingual and manual caress in widely separated timespace locations. But there is no clear doctrine about what the conditions of the possibility for this might be. Formally speaking, it must be the case that the ascended flesh isn't subject to metronomic time or map-gridded space. This formal requirement can be speculatively glossed in many ways. Among them is the attractive thought that, with the resurrection and the consequent ascension, the folding of timespace around the flesh of Jesus is, in the metronomic temporal order measurable by clocks, increasingly evident. That speculation suggests a further one, close to the heart of Christian orthodoxy, which is that the incarnation, the taking of flesh on the part of the triune LORD in the person of the Word, is itself an atemporal fact, a state of affairs belonging timelessly to the trinitarian economy; that time has always, atemporally, been coiled around or folded upon that fleshly triunity; and that the invisibility of that folding characteristic of time's metronomic passage (just one damn thing after another, ending always in death) is now, since the ascension, being visibly attenuated. Time is being healed, its distensive stretching out into past and future being returned to what it was, is, and will be, which is a systolic-diastolic cycle centered upon the flesh of Jesus—and the principal evidence of that healing is the real presence of the ascended flesh outside the measures of metronomic time. When the flesh of those cleaved to Jesus's flesh in baptism consumes the ascended flesh of Jesus in the eucharist, that Jesus-cleaved flesh performs what is most appropriate for it and participates thereby, as temporal creatures can, in the atemporal life of the Trinity.

The work of Jesus's ascended flesh is made clearest, scripturally, in the Johannine literature. Jesus's natal flesh is a central topic of the prologue to John's Gospel: *verbum caro factum est*; and the resurrected flesh is more fully presented in that Gospel than in any of the others (2.4). It is also in that Gospel that the ascended flesh is described most fully. Consider the following passages, from John's sixth chapter:

> Your ancestors [Jesus is speaking to the Jews] ate manna in the desert and died. This is the bread that comes down from heaven (*de caelo descendens*) so that those who eat from that very thing won't die. I am the living bread who came down from heaven (*de caelo descendi*). Anyone who eats from this bread will live forever—for the bread I will give is my flesh for the world's life (*caro mea est pro mundi vita*).

Even manna, the LORD's gift of food outside the ordinary gustatory economy of work and killing to the wandering and starving people of Israel, doesn't prevent death. The *panis vivus* (living bread), by contrast, brings life with it, life not subject to death. The sequence of tenses is instructive: first, the living bread came down from heaven—past tense; then, Jesus says that the bread he will give (future tense, *dabo*) is his flesh (*caro*), and that those who eat it will live (*vivet*, future tense) forever. The same sequence persists here:

> . . . unless you will have eaten (*manducaveritis*) the Son of Man's flesh and will have drunk (*biberitis*) his blood, you have no life in you. Those who eat my flesh and drink my blood have eternal life (*habet vitam aeternam*), and I will raise (*resuscitabo*) them on the last day (*novissimo die*)—for my flesh is true food and my blood true drink. Those who eat (*manducat*) my flesh and drink (*bibit*) my blood remain in me (*in me manet*), and I in them. Just as (*sicut*) the living Father sent (*misit*) me and I live because of the Father, so those who eat me will themselves live (*vivet*) because of me. This is the bread of life which came down (*descendit*) from heaven; it's not like what your ancestors ate, and died. Those who eat (*manducat*) this bread will live (*vivet*) forever.

Jesus's followers will, in order to have (present tense) eternal life (eternal present tense), have to have done (future perfect) something—which is to say, eaten his flesh and drunk his blood, which, at the time of this discourse, aren't yet available, and at the time when they will be (future) raised, again won't be available, but which in the interim will be (and from the viewpoint of the eternal-present consummation will have been). John is writing of the ascended flesh, at once restrospectively and anticipatorily. He's also careful to distinguish it from the natal flesh: that's what descended (past tense) when Jesus was conceived, and what now speaks. And so, lapidarily, those who eat this bread (like us, who can do so now) will live forever. That—being edible without the constraints of timespace—is the work of the ascended flesh, and it's only in being ascended, in being unavailable to our senses in locatable human form, that the ascended flesh can do this work.

It isn't, however, that this is the only work the ascended flesh does. That flesh stands (or sits) at the Father's right hand, as both Scripture and creed affirm. And, for Catholics at least, that flesh is not alone: it is with, accompanied by, Mary's assumed flesh. Pius XII defined the dogma of Mary's assumption in 1950, in *Munificentissimus Deus*, and as part of that definition used the following formulation: *Immaculatam Deiparam semper Virginem Mariam, expleto terrestris vitae cursu, fuisse corpore et anima ad caelestem gloriam assumptam*—Mary, ever-virgin and immaculate mother of God, when she had completed the course of her earthly life was assumed body and soul into heavenly glory. Earlier in the same document, Pius mentions with approval Bernardine of Siena's view that Mary must be where Jesus is, and that it is proper that she should be there as he is, which is to say in soul and body. Pius's definition doesn't use the term "flesh" (*caro*), but rather "body" (*corpus*), but this doesn't at all affect the fundamental point of the definition, which is that Mary's flesh is where Jesus's ascended flesh is—and that this is true now, in the order of metronomic time, and not something to be awaited.

Mary's flesh may not be the only flesh accompanying Jesus's ascended flesh. In the fifth chapter of Genesis Enoch vanishes *quia tulit eum deus*—because god took him, while he was walking with god (*ambulavitque cum deo*). Scripture doesn't elaborate, and when the later tradition, Jewish and Christian, does (it often does, and at length), it typically says that Enoch doesn't die but is taken in the flesh to be with the LORD. If that's the correct interpretation, then Enoch's flesh, too, like Mary's, is with Jesus's ascended flesh. Elijah, too, as the account in the second chapter of the Second Book of Kings has it, is taken up into heaven (*et ascendit Elias per turbinem in caelum*) without dying, which may imply that his flesh, too, is with Jesus's ascended flesh in heaven.

With respect to the fleshly presence of Mary in heaven, the central points are two. First, her fleshly presence there accords with the principle that she ought to be where he (Jesus) is, and ought to be where he is as he is, which is to say incarnately. Pius XII's thought suggests (and in this he follows many earlier theologians) that this principle exhibits *convenientia*, appropriateness and beauty. That isn't why it's true, but it is why it seems to Christians to be true: it harmonizes with and deepens the order of the faith. The second point is that a full account of Jesus's ascended flesh requires discussion not only of the eucharistic presence of that flesh, but also of its heavenly presence and the company it keeps there. Elijah's and Enoch's presence there (if that's the right account) underscores this point, and the thought that eventually, when timespace is healed and creatures find themselves in it as flesh in intimate fleshly—and therefore tactile—relation to Jesus's flesh, there'll be much more company, underscores it still more. Salvation is a matter of the flesh, and it involves human flesh as much as the flesh of Jesus. "Heaven" is a timespace label for the there/then of a mode of fleshly relation.

But what might a full(er) account of this aspect of the ascended flesh be like? It's easier to be negative than positive on that point. Heaven is not a timespace according to the metronome or the map grid. It can't be arrived at by timespace movement so understood, and the upward metaphor (*ascendere*) of scriptural and traditional discussions of the ascension isn't a metaphor of that kind; it signals, rather, a definitive mode of absence, which is to say a mode of presence that is in no respect under the sign of the metronome and the map grid. None of this is a contingent matter, either; heaven is by definition not spatiotemporally locatable, and that's because healed (redeemed) timespace is what heaven is, and timespace in that mode is not locatable in those ways. In positive mode: heaven is where/when the ascended flesh of Jesus is; it's the timespace in which fleshly creatures keep closely intimate company with the ascended flesh, where the lingual (and, sometimes, manual) caress under which intimacy with Jesus's ascended flesh occurs here below, in the eucharistic communion of metronomic timespace, is supplemented by interaction with all the other senses. There and then Jesus's human flesh will be visible, audible, and smellable, just as here and now it can be taste-touched. Haptic relations to that ascended and human-formed flesh will then also be complete in ways that exceed the imagination.

A very imperfect imaginative avenue into that intimacy may perhaps be found by considering what the most comprehensive tactile embrace is like here and now. That most comprehensive embrace occurs in the womb: there, the baby's flesh is embraced at every point, without remainder, by the mother's flesh. None of us recalls what that was like, but it is hard not to think that it must have been delightful—a cleaving of unmatched intimacy—and that its loss must have been agonizing and fundamentally disorienting. The haptic fleshly intimacy that resurrected flesh will have with Jesus's ascended flesh will be like that, only more so. Since our births, our wrenching from womb flesh, we've had only partial and still more imperfect anticipations of what we hope for. We have, sometimes, been closely embraced by human flesh: we've been, if lucky, folded into our mother's arms, have sucked at her breasts, have been enwrapped by our lovers, and have had one or another fleshly part of ours inside the flesh of another, or one or another of their fleshly parts inside ours—penis in vagina, tongue in mouth, and so on (6.1–6.4). But that's all. Since birth, and before resurrection, it isn't possible for every inch of someone's skin at one and the same time to exchange touch with every inch of another's, which is the unreachable goal of every caress. Something is always untouched, and the human need, often desperate, for caresses suggests how deep is the craving for fleshly touch that is complete and without remainder. That we can only have from Jesus's ascended flesh. Beyond that, probably, speculation cannot go.

This line of eschatological thought about the work of Jesus's ascended flesh properly corrects and completes the thought that the relations between human resurrected flesh and the LORD are essentially a matter of vision. That, after all, is had by the separated soul, which is (for Catholic orthodoxy) temporarily discarnate; if, as Catholic orthodoxy also requires, there is fleshly resurrection consequent upon the soul's separation from the flesh at death, then the difference between what the separated soul knows of the triune LORD and what the resurrected person—flesh and soul—knows of the triune LORD must be given by the flesh, and by the nature of its relations to the ascended flesh of Jesus. There is no other difference to find.

These speculations about fleshly touch are a way of specifying the difference between what resurrected persons know of the LORD, and what separated souls and enfleshed persons prior to death know of the LORD. Before death, creaturely flesh that's been cleaved to Jesus Christ in baptism can have a real but limited fleshly intimacy with the ascended LORD through the eucharist. It can also have a real but darkened and constrained understanding of the LORD through partial intellectual vision. After death, but before the resurrection, the separated soul deepens its intellectual vision of the LORD, approaching in this what the angels have as a matter of course, and thus beginning to participate in the beatific vision; but it has no fleshly intimacy of any kind with the LORD because it is discarnate, which is at least to say that the eucharistic touch of the LORD's ascended flesh ceases with death. After the resurrection, the intellectual vision of the LORD is completed by a full fleshly intimacy with the LORD's ascended flesh, an intimacy that extends and deepens what could be had by way of the eucharist here below, and that is coupled with the intellectual vision already possessed by the discarnate soul in the intermediate state. It's at this point, the moment of the general resurrection, that Jesus becomes all in all, one part of the meaning of which is that his ascended flesh ceases to be available eucharistically, and occupies its last locus, which is also its supremely and definitively new (*novissimum*) locus, at the right hand of the Father and at the center of the assembly of the resurrected. Then and there, much company is kept, and all of it fleshly.

3 FLESH CLEAVED

IS THERE SUCH A THING as Christian flesh? On the one hand it seems not, because all humans are fleshly, and the fleshliness of Christians is not distinct from that of other humans. Nothing available to the senses marks Christian flesh in such a way as to distinguish it from other human flesh. What makes Christians fleshly, therefore—what their flesh is and appears to be—is just what makes other human creatures fleshly. There is no distinctively Christian flesh; whatever it is that distinguishes Christians from non-Christians has nothing to do with their flesh.

But against this, Jesus was and is flesh, and because of who he was and is he serves as the paradigm of all human flesh. His flesh is fully human, though without sin, and it therefore shows what human flesh most properly is, how it is configured and what it does when it is as it should be. That is in the order of being: all human flesh participates, as human flesh, in Jesus's flesh; it is given its form and meaning by that participation and is therefore in that sense Christian. Human flesh as such is therefore also Christian flesh. There can be no human flesh that is not also Christian flesh. It is proper to the grammar of the faith to say so, and so saying provides the first meaning of "Christian flesh."

This is true so far as it goes. But the position so stated identifies nothing distinctive about Christian flesh as a sub-kind of human flesh. Rather, it gives sense to the phrase "Christian flesh" by identifying all human flesh as partici- pant in Christ's flesh: it redescribes the category of human flesh, but doesn't subdivide it. Is there a meaning of "Christian flesh" that identifies some humans as bearing it (being borne by it), and others not? And that does so by identifying the distinguishing marks of Christian flesh?

Perhaps. All human creatures are by definition fleshly. Without flesh, no human creature. The separated soul, which Catholic Christians (and some others) affirm can and does exist independently of the flesh, and begins to do so at the moment of the flesh's return to body in death, while it is certainly something, and while it is lineally and intimately related to the human creature of which it is a proper constituent, is not itself a human creature. To be human is to be fleshly, and that grammatical claim—that it is a misuse of the term "human" to separate what it designates from the flesh, just as much as it is to separate what it designates from the soul—means that to attend to human creatures requires attention to the flesh that in part constitutes them. To think that human creatures might be simply spiritual, simply soulish, makes it possible for them to exist discarnately; but they cannot. To think that human creatures might be simply fleshly, simply contiguously extended in timespace, makes it possible for them to exist as corpses; but they cannot. A corpse is not a human creature, and neither is a discarnate soul. A human creature is living flesh of a particular kind, ensouled (animate) in a particular way.

All humans are fleshly, but not all here below in the devastation are Christian. Those who are Christian, a subset of the whole, are by definition so in a fleshly sense; there's no other way in which they could be Christian. "Christian flesh," therefore, as a phrase, labels just and only those who are Christian. "Christian" is synecdoche for "Christian flesh." Whatever it is that makes Christians here below what they are is also what makes their flesh Christian and themselves, therefore, Christian flesh, fleshly in a Christian sense. If being Christian meant nothing for their flesh, then it would mean nothing for them. It would be surd. The question is not whether there is such a thing as Christian flesh; there is and must be if there are Christians. The question is only what marks that flesh in the order of being, and what marks it in the order of knowing: what does human flesh become when it becomes Christian? And what are the marks by which it can be recognized as Christian?

First, and most fundamentally, Christian flesh is baptized flesh. The baptized are made intimate with Christ's flesh. The baptismal liturgies and Scripture tend to put this by saying not that the baptized have become members of Christ's flesh, but that they are now members of his body. This is an instance of the difference, and the tension, between flesh-talk and body-talk in Christian discourse. The *sarx/soma* and *caro/corpus* pairs, like the flesh/body pair in

English, have different patterns of use, but the differences are not marked with precision, and while it is often not possible to substitute "flesh" for "body" (it sounds, and is, malformed to say "the Word became body," or that "He became body from the Virgin Mary"), sometimes such a substitution can be made. The baptized are incorporated into him, made members of him, clothed with him, have their flesh touched—embraced—by his—eventually, clearly, when they eat his flesh in the eucharist, for which baptism is a necessary condition, but also already in baptism, when they are chrismated, exsufflated, laved, and illuminated. Christian flesh understood as baptized flesh is, therefore, in the order of being more intimate with the flesh of Jesus than it is with non-Christian (Jewish, pagan) flesh. By distant, but real, analogy: spouses are more intimate with one another's flesh than they are with anyone else's. The same is true, though not in the same way, of the relation between a mother's flesh and the flesh of her children, and, differently again, of the relation between a father's flesh and the flesh of his children. Intimacy comes in degrees and kinds, and Christian flesh is, according to this line of reasoning, distinguished from non-Christian flesh precisely by the degree of its intimacy with Jesus's flesh.

Christian flesh is made what it is by baptism: it descends into the water of baptism as one kind of flesh and rises, reborn, as another. Its new status as clothed with Christ is sealed by chrismation and represented by the white baptismal garment. The flesh of the baptized is marked as Christ's own forever, as many baptismal liturgies have it, and this mark, unavailable to the senses, cannot be erased. Once baptized, always baptized; once marked, always marked; once a Christian, always a Christian. It is a remarkable feature of Christianity that, in this sense at least, there is no exit—no rite that marks exit, and no concept available for the idea of exit. Christianity is, like being the child of particular parents, a condition that once entered upon cannot be left behind. It's also a condition in which there is no hierarchy and no distinction. That is, all Christians—all the baptized—are equally so. Baptism is a toggle concept rather than a spectrum concept: on or off, in or out, the same for all, Jew, Greek, male, female, slave, free.

But this doesn't mean that the transformative effects of baptism are equally present, and even much less so that they are equally evident, in all the baptized. To have become something new, and to have become so irreversibly, doesn't entail that the newness in question is insulated from obscurity, occlusion, corruption, damage, or forgetfulness. The baptized may not know, and may never have known, that they are baptized; they may once have known but have now

forgotten; their white garment may have become so soiled by acts that speak
against the baptism that gave it to them that its whiteness is no longer apparent to them or to anyone else—other than the triune LORD, to whom it, like
everything else, is apparent without remainder. All this means that even though
there are modes of fleshly action properly characteristic of Christian (baptized)
flesh, and, concomitantly, modes of such action that actively speak against what
that flesh now is, and even though an accurate account of what is proper to
Christian flesh's actions in particular spheres often differs significantly from
an accurate account of what is proper to non-Christian flesh's actions in those
same spheres, it is not the case that particular Christians always or even usually
act in accord with what they are.

So, the second answer to the question of whether there is such a thing as
Christian flesh addresses its actions, and is affirmative—unlike in the case of
its form, markings, adornments, or coverings. In the order of being, the fleshly
acts of Christians are distinctive not because of what they are—the full and ordinary range of human fleshly acts is available to the baptized, and all of them
are performed—but because of their double possibility. Some among these acts
glorify the LORD by conformity to the nature of the flesh that performs them;
and some among them performatively contradict—speak against—the nature
of the flesh that performs them. Christian flesh is conceptually distinguishable
from non-Christian flesh by the givenness of its participation in and conformity to Christ. Baptism has made it different, and the nature of that difference
can be specified.

3.1   Cleaving

Cleaving is an intimate fleshly attachment constituted by touch. Those who
cleave embrace, clasp, hug, caress, or ingest what they cleave to; they enter into
it, or allow it entry into them; cleavings are a matter of close haptic joining,
flesh to body or flesh to flesh. Such intimacies are no light matter; most flesh is
kept at a distance beyond touch because cleavings are, and are understood to
be, dangerous and important: they hurt those who engage in them as often as
they nourish them, and in both cases deeply; and they show, often disturbingly,
how deep the need for cleaving is, and how broad the range of things, bodies
and flesh, to which cleaving can be sought. Human cleavings need, therefore,
close attention and careful regulation, and they receive both. Once formed by

the pressures of the social and natural worlds, no one ingests or caresses or embraces just anything; everyone, instead, is observant and careful of haptic intimacy. When cleaving is forced, by violence or other pressures (unwanted food thrust down the throat, unwanted flesh brought close to or inside one's own), the result is both a sense of violation and an actual violation. Also, because human flesh is given its location in the social world by its cleavings—things eaten, things worn, things caressed—it is constantly threatened with sanction if it cleaves to the wrong things or to the right things in the wrong ways. Punishment, sometimes violent, follows from eating the wrong thing, caressing or entering forbidden flesh, and allowing tabooed bodies or flesh entry into one's own. Haptic intimacy, cleaving, is carefully guarded, therefore, and especially so when it's a matter of cleaving, and being cloven, to the flesh of other human creatures.

Cleaving, among humans, can be a one-to-one relation, and when it is it brings into being a couple: clasped, adhering, haptically intimate, in close caress; making love or holding hands; salving the other's flesh or having one's own salved; carrying or being carried; bare-handedly strangling or being strangled. It can also be a relation that haptically binds the members of a group, and when it is it brings into being a multi-membered fleshly conglomerate: a conga line, a parent simultaneously embracing several children, the members of a jubilant sports team group-hugging. Cleaving can be violent or loving, creative or destructive. It can nurture and heal and bind cleaved flesh, and it can as easily damage and destroy it. In either case, the means is haptic intimacy: cleaving. The torturer and the tortured are cleaved as much as the lover and the beloved.

Cleaving is, first, a kind of joining. But the verb, to cleave, also indicates division, usually violent, as when one thing is harshly sundered from another. In this sense, the crusader cleaves the infidel's head from his shoulders, perhaps crying *Christus dominus est* while doing so; the carpenter's hammer and chisel cleave a teak board along the grain, making two of one; a sandstone massif is cleft by a river's millennia-long erosive force causing a cleavage, a valley dividing the redrock landscape. The same (in pronunciation, in spelling) English verb is used for both violent division and intimate haptic attachment. There is a historical explanation for this: two verbs distinct in etymology and meaning came, by the fourteenth century or so, to have the same spelling and pronunciation and, for the most part, the same inflections to indicate tense, mood, person, and number. The verb is a contronym, a word that bears two opposed meanings (there are many of these in English), and dictionaries often treat contronyms as if they were two different words, accidentally homophonic and contingently orthographically indistinguishable, but really distinct.

That is a possible approach. Historians and lexicographers find it attractive. But it obscures the fact that averagely fluent users of English, spoken and written, hear and see echoes of division, more or less violent, when "cleave" is used in the haptic-intimacy sense, and they see and hear echoes of fleshly intimacy when "cleave" is used in the sudden-sundering sense. Cloven intimacy comes with undertones and suggestions of cleft division, as does cloven separation with implications of cleft joining. The cleft stick and the cloven hoof bring the two ranges of meaning together. The hoof and the stick are one, though divided; and their divisions—the stick's branching, the hoof's bifurcation—are haptically intimate one with another. The hoof and stick as a whole are divided and joined; and joined exactly as divided.

The first sense of "to cleave" (intimate haptic attachment) is inevitably inflected by the second (sundering of what was once joined) in the order of being, and it's useful to keep this inflection in mind in the order of thinking. In the human sphere, intimate haptic attachment presupposes and ends in sundering, and sundering requires a prior haptic connection. The child's flesh in the womb is as cleaved (first sense) as possible to the mother's flesh; but that cleaving (first sense) is inevitably followed by a violent cleaving (second sense) of the one from the other marked, drastically, by exit through the birth canal and the cutting of the umbilicus. Lovers entwined haptically cleave (first sense), but were previously separated in the flesh and will, sooner or later, have even their most intimate and extended embraces cleft (second sense). The strangler, thumbs compressing the victim's windpipe, is haptically intimate with the victim's flesh, and deeply so; but that cleaving (first sense) is rapidly followed by a cleaving (second sense) of the murderer's flesh from the victim's as the victim, asphyxiated, falls dead.

Haptic intimacy is shadowed always by sundering. Separation is its point of origin and separation its end, and the felt fabric of fleshly joinings (cleaving first sense) contains the anticipation of the sundering of those joinings (cleaving second sense). The semantic range of the (single) verb "to cleave" in English embraces this situation; it is an especially clear case of what seems at first sight to be sheer linguistic contingency—two separate verbs coalescing by accident— yielding, and perhaps being produced by, a real linguistic and conceptual need. Cleavings, here, are close haptic attachments framed by and intimate at once with the fact of their inevitable sundering and the sense of that sundering entwined already with the sense of what it's like to be joined in the flesh. That only one verb is needed to do that work is a gift and a delight.

In the sixth chapter of his first letter to the Corinthians, Paul writes about cleaving (*adhaerere*) like this:

> "Everything's permitted to me." But not everything's expedient. "Everything's permitted to me." But I'll be brought under the power of nothing. "Food for the belly and the belly for foods." But God will destroy it and them. The body, however, isn't for fornication but for the LORD, and the LORD for the body; God has certainly raised the LORD and will raise us by his power. Don't you know that your bodies are Christ's limbs? Should I then take Christ's limbs and make them into a prostitute's? Absolutely not. Don't you know that someone who cleaves to a prostitute is one body? For *they will be*, he said, *two in one flesh*. But someone who cleaves to the LORD is one spirit. Abandon fornication. Whatever sin someone might commit is done outside the body, but fornicators sin in their own bodies. Don't you know that your body is a temple of the Holy Spirit who is in you and whom you have from God, and that you aren't your own? You've been bought with a price. Therefore glorify God in your own body.

According to this text, humans have, or are, a body of flesh with limbs (*membra*)—legs, arms, eyes, feet, hands, head, penis, vagina, belly, breasts, buttocks, throat, tongue, teeth, and so on. If they are Christian, their flesh, as a whole and in its parts, belongs to Christ; it is his because they—they as flesh— have been bought with a price (*empti enim estis pretio*); and the sense in which their flesh is his and not their own (*non estis vestri*) is given principally by the verb "to cleave" (*adhaerere*). "Someone who cleaves to a prostitute is one body . . . someone who cleaves to the LORD is one spirit" (*qui adhaeret meretrici, unum corpus est . . . qui autem adhaeret Domino, unus spiritus est*). Christians are glued to Jesus's flesh, stuck on it, brought into it, made participant in it. They are in it and it is in them. They and it—they and he—are, now, having cleaved, one spirit; and that Spirit, the Holy Spirit, is in them—in their flesh and each of its parts—which makes their flesh a temple of and for that Spirit, which in turn is Jesus's spirit because it proceeds from him as well as from the Father. Their flesh's limbs are, now, analogically and participatorily, Jesus's—*corpora vestra membra Christi sunt*. What they do with them is what he does with his. What he does with his, which now include theirs and them, is partly constituted by what they do with theirs. Their fleshly agency and his are no longer cleanly separable. They, now, should glorify God in their own bodies (*glorificate ergo deum in corpore vestro*): the verb is imperative, which is to say that they're being asked (demanded, encouraged, required) to do this, to carry Jesus around with, in, and as, their flesh; but it is possible to respond to the imperative only because what it asks is the case. Their flesh is his; his is in them; they cleave to him with a depth of ingression and an irreversible intimacy that other fleshly ingressions and intimacies (eating, sex, pregnancy, parasitic invasion, symbiotic dependency) can only intimate, imitate, and (sometimes) speak against. Jesus's flesh is closer to theirs than anyone else's—closer than spousal flesh, than children's flesh, than lovers' flesh, than the flesh of the bacteria in the gut—because Christians are, now, in every fleshly part and in every fleshly action, his and him.

—But, in considering the theological implications of Scripture's lexical specificities—the presence, in this case, of the verb "to cleave" in Paul's Corinthian correspondence—isn't it strange to focus with such semantic intensity on English and Latin? Isn't Greek the language Paul used in composing this correspondence, and isn't it therefore better to consider the semantic and conceptual baggage of the words Paul actually used rather than renderings of them into other languages? Isn't, therefore, this analysis of cleaving fundamentally misconceived? Oughtn't it be replaced with an analysis of the Greek verb *kollaō*? Or oughtn't it at least be acknowledged that the semantic range of *adhaerere* and that of "to cleave" aren't the same?

—Not exactly. This objection is based on a faulty understanding of Scriptural authority. Renderings of Paul's Greek into other languages are also the LORD's word. It's a fundamental Christian commitment that the canon of Scripture can be translated without loss of its capacity to address Christians as the LORD's word—Christian liturgical habits show this to be the case, as when Christians elevate the scriptural book during worship and call it *verbum Domini*, no matter what language it's being read in. Reading Paul in Latin or English isn't second best to reading him in Greek; likewise with attending to the lexical specificities of Paul in English, or any other language. In the case of particular word choices, this is especially true when a particular rendering has a long history and a broad liturgical and ecclesial use, as is the case with "to cleave."

Paul also, in this passage from the Corinthian correspondence, likens the relation between Christian flesh and Jesus's flesh to that between temples and the LORD. Temples house the LORD. In housing the LORD, they bear the LORD in themselves; the LORD is their inhabitant, and the LORD's presence glorifies them inevitably, transfigures them in all their particulars no matter what those particulars are. The flesh of Christians is the same. Transfigured, like it or not; Christ's, like it or not; a Spirit-temple, like it or not; radiant with the LORD's presence, like it or not; and all that no matter what its shape, color, size, sex, age, health, and so on. But temples—the LORD's houses— nevertheless do and should look different from houses that aren't temples. Scripture certainly suggests this. It gives a lot of attention to the construction of the Ark of the Covenant, and still more to the dimensions and decoration of the first and second temples in Jerusalem. That attention has to do with glorification. The temple's appearance should glorify the LORD, ought to be at least a pale reflection of the fact that the LORD inhabits it. And these shoulds and oughts mean that temples look different from houses that aren't temples. As with synagogues, in this respect, so also with churches. They are tabernacles: places where the LORD can be found in ways not true of other houses, places in which the LORD's flesh lives, eucharistically and in the flesh of the baptized. The LORD's glory isn't evenly distributed in the world; the world is rough ground in this respect as in every other.

Extending this thought to the flesh as the Spirit's—and Jesus's—temple is difficult, though. There is and should be nothing about the configuration or adornment of Christian flesh that marks it to the eye as what it is. No circumcision, no tattoos, no amputations, no distinctive clothing, no particular hairstyles— nothing at all like that. Christians, in these respects, are unlike Jews, Sikhs, Hindus, and so on, but rather more like Buddhists, whose flesh is also unmarked to the eye. Christian flesh is, while resting and whether naked or clothed, invisible as such to the eye, whether that eye is Christian or pagan or Jewish. But if the temple analogy does any work, there ought nonetheless to be some distinctives. Christian flesh ought to show what it is to the world, ought to make its glorification of the LORD evident: *glorificate ergo deum in corpore vestro*—glorify, therefore, God in your body. The clue is in the limbs: *nescitis quoniam corpora vestra membra Christi sunt?*—don't you know that your bodies are Christ's limbs? The limbs are the flesh in action: our legs and feet walk and run, our lips and tongues kiss and speak, our hands and fingers make and unmake. When Christian flesh glorifies the LORD, it acts in accord with what it is; when it does not—and that the verb, glorify, is imperative shows that it might not, as does saying that fornication (*fornicatio*) contradicts Christian flesh—it speaks against what it is by what it does. The distinctively temple-like nature of Christian flesh is evident, when it is and to the extent that it is, not in what it looks like but in what it does, how it acts in the world. Some actions reduce it, making it less; others show it for what it is.

If being cleaved to someone or something means, in part, haptic intimacy, then being cloven to Jesus's flesh, which is what this passage from Paul's correspondence with the Corinthians treats, means touching Jesus, being close to him in the flesh. This seems odd at first blush. Jesus's flesh is ascended and sits now at the right hand of the Father, where it can be neither seen nor touched. How, then, can there be haptic intimacy with it, cleaving to it? The answer is twofold. First, his flesh is touched in the eucharist by eating and drinking (2.5); that's a peculiarly intimate touch and, therefore, a peculiarly intimate kind of cleaving. Ingesting Jesus forms Christian flesh, and does so over time as does all ingestion. The absence of his ascended flesh in any form other than the consecrated elements of the eucharist does not, therefore, prevent haptic intimacies. But there is more. By baptism Christian flesh is placed in a relation with Jesus's flesh that makes haptic intimacy with him a constant feature of its life. Christian flesh has put on Christ, is clothed with Christ, its (fleshly) members are Christ's, and so on. These figures all suggest deep and constant haptic intimacy, a cleaving that can be sundered, certainly, but that is real, really fleshly, and, therefore, properly to be labelled as cleaving. This cleaving, that of haptic intimacy with the flesh of Christ, is the deepest and most thoroughgoing that Christians can have; like all cleavings, it is shadowed by violent separation, but unlike all other cleavings, separation can only be brought about by the decision and action of the Christian. From the side of Jesus, which is the same as to say from the side of the triune LORD, no sundering can occur. The baptized are marked as Christ's own for ever; and this means that haptic intimacy with Jesus's flesh can never be fully and finally removed even though it can be seriously damaged by sin.

3.2   Fornication

Some fleshly cleavings that Christians seek glorify the LORD and sit well with Christian flesh as Jesus-cleaved. But others speak against that condition, and these are fornicatory cleavings. These are cleavings also possible for Christian flesh, and they come, for Christian flesh, in two kinds: idolatrous and scandalous.

Idolatrous cleavings first. When Christians cleave idolatrously they don't cleave to real idols, for there are none. Rather, idolatrous cleavings are adverbial: when Christians cleave idolatrously they join their flesh to creatures in ways that speak against the goodness of what they cleave to and against the goodness that belongs to the fleshly intimacies in which cleaving consists. Anything that can be cleaved to—the flesh of another human creature; the flesh of a nonhuman animal; an inanimate object—is, simply by virtue of its existence, a creaturely good. To cleave to any such thing is, therefore, to cleave to a good. Similarly, all creaturely cleavings, fleshly intimacies established by some creature with another, are necessarily good, good by definition. Fleshly intimacy is what flesh is made for; it's only by exchanging such intimacies that it can be established as flesh. Considered simply as such, cleavings have in them nothing but good. None can be placed under the ban.

How is it then that not all cleavings sit well with Jesus-cleaved flesh? How is it that some, in their performance, speak directly against what such flesh is? If not because of their objects (everything is permitted), and not because of anything wrong with cleaving as such (again, everything is permitted), cleavings that speak against Jesus-cleaved flesh must do so because of the way in which the cleaving is done. To cleave idolatrously is to take what you cleave to as an idol, to cleave to it as if it were a good independent of its creator, a self-standing uncreated good. Any such thing is a phantasm: there are no self-standing uncreated goods save the triune LORD. To seek fleshly intimacy with a phantasm is a peculiarly incoherent act: when you seek to cleave idolatrously with something, the fact that you understand what you're caressing as an idol precisely guarantees that you can have no fleshly intimacy with it. Caresses given to a phantasm fail as caresses, even when they look like caresses given to real flesh.

You can do some things with phantasms, however. It's not that they're altogether beyond the possibility of relation.

One thing you can do is to dominate the phantasm, become to it as a little lord, a *dominus* on a small scale. Phantasms lend themselves to this. Surgeons, defeated by the scale and intractability of damage undergone by real flesh on the operating table before them, which they try to heal and cannot, may imagine, later, flesh that would have yielded itself to their healing hands, flesh that their hands would have healed. That flesh is a phantasm, and because of that it yields itself perfectly and fully to the surgeons' fleshly intimacy. Real flesh, too, can become a phantasm in the hands of the surgeon, and it does so to the extent that its creaturely goodness and integrity are taken from it by the surgical gesture. It might be tested to destruction, sliced to death, or fatally infected. Those acts require the caress (now tending toward the wound), but it is a caress directed only in part toward real flesh; what it really seeks is an idol for domination, and when it treats what it seeks to cleave to in that way it fails to establish real intimacy. Its gesture is self-defeating.

Another thing you can do with a phantasm is bring it to nothing. That is not possible with created goods. They are what they are because the LORD made them, and they cannot simply be removed from existence. Animate creatures can be killed and inanimate ones disaggregated or otherwise subjected to damage. But those are not, as Christians see it, acts that bring creatures to nothing; rather, such acts temporarily interrupt the presence in metronomic and map-gridded timespace of the creatures to which they are done. Phantasms, though, have only the existence imagined for them by their idolizers, and that kind of existence can, without remainder, be brought to nothing. If you idolize the flesh of your beloved by imagining it as perfect and perfectly responsive to your desire, you can bring that idol to nothing. When things go well between you and your beloved, and you begin to see the beloved's flesh as real, which is to say as belonging to the beloved and therefore neither perfect nor fully responsive to your desire, then your idolization of it may begin to vanish before its reality; and if, as almost never happens here below, your cleavings to the beloved become, without remainder, cleavings to a person and not to an idol, then it may be that you'll have brought your idol to nothing. The process can move in the opposite direction, too, and when it does your beloved's flesh is progressively overcome by your cleavings to your idol. Eventually, it may be, real flesh is of no more interest to you; you come to want only the kind that is sought idolatrously, and then you'll abandon or kill your beloved.

Fornications of the idolatrous kind are, then, attempts to cleave that guarantee their own failure by imagining an object with which no fleshly intimacy is possible. Domination and removal are what idolatrous fornications make possible; fleshly intimacy is what they rule out. Short of heaven, and perhaps also the garden before the fall, all actual cleavings are in part idolatrous. None is altogether free of phantasms: whenever an apple's flesh is bitten into and chewed, what's in the mouth is always in part treated idolatrously; likewise when the beloved's flesh is caressed.

What now of scandalous fornications? Those, like all fornications, are cleavings that speak against Christian flesh. They differ from idolatrous fornications by not being, on the part of those who seek and perform them, especially idolatrous. They may be mostly alive to the particularity and reality and recalcitrance of the flesh being cleaved to, and thus only minimally idolatrous. What makes them fornications is something different. It is that in light of local and contingent social arrangements they can move the imaginations of others, those who observe these cleavings rather than those performing them, idolwards. Suppose you, cleaved to Jesus in baptism, are often observed, by those who know what a member of the Ku Klux Klan is and wears, dressing as one; suppose you, likewise cleaved, are seen to eat the flesh of tortured animals by those who know what animal torture is and that this flesh you're consuming is just such a corpse; or, suppose you're seen by those who know what industrial-scale prostution is and means, seeking fleshly intimacy with those employed by that very industry. These are all fleshly cleavings: clothing the flesh in a particular way, ingesting matter into the flesh, caressing flesh other than your own. You may or may not be performing these intimacies idolatrously, as fornications of that type. But because of local institutional arrangements having to do with the meaning of uniforms, the modes of meat production, and the methods of commercializing sexual caresses, you are cleaving scandalously.

"Scandal" here means an occasion of damage to others. When Christian flesh cleaves in ways that damage those not directly involved in its cleavings, it does so scandalously. And scandalous cleavings are also fornications because they do not sit well with Christian flesh. They speak against it as cleaved to Jesus because they can cause observers to conclude that the cleavings they're observing are imitable, when in fact they may be damaging to those who have not (yet) cleaved to Jesus.

Idolatrously fornicatory cleavings can be difficult to discriminate from cleavings that glorify the LORD, and that is because what makes such fornications idolatrous is neither the gestures of intimacy nor the creatures with whom intimacy is sought, but rather the purposive imaginations of those doing the fornicating. Scandalously fornicatory cleavings are still harder to discriminate from glorificatory ones because the scandalous ones become scandalous—give scandal—only when particular local institutional arrangements are in place and are known to be so. Wearing a white hood and mask, by itself, is not at all a fornicatory cleaving to clothes; it becomes scandalous only when there's been a particular history, and when that history is known. That is why there can be no simple list of scandalous fornications—scandalous caresses (6.4), scandalous eatings (5.6), scandalous modes of dress (4.6). They can be defined only formally: a particular seeking of fleshly intimacy is scandalous when, and to the extent that, it moves the imaginations and actions of those who observe it toward idolatrous cleavings.

Paul's discussion of cleaving in his first letter to the Corinthians (3.1) also uses "fornication" (*fornicatio*) to label a kind of cleaving incompatible with cleaving to Jesus. To fornicate, he writes there, is to cleave to a prostitute, a *meretrix*—perhaps a temple prostitute, one whose sexual services are dedicated to an idol. When Christians undertake this meretricious joining of limbs, they do something that, even if permitted (*omnia mihi licent*), is not expedient. Why not? Because it speaks against the nature of flesh that has cleaved to Jesus. The one act of cleaving—gluing, sticking, entering, participating—is not compatible with the other. They are noncomposible: Christian flesh, Jesus-cleaved, Spirit-inhabited, speaks against itself when it cleaves to prostitutes, especially those dedicated to the service of idols. The contradiction is fleshly, and paradigmatically so; it's one undertaken in and with one's own flesh (*qui autem fornicatur in corpus suum peccat*—fornicators, who sin in their own bodies), and in this is different from sins undertaken outside the flesh—sins of intention and motivation. Fornicators do not glorify the LORD in their flesh; they occlude the LORD's glory and indicate, by their action, their fleshly conformity and subjection to something—someone—other than the LORD. So to act is performatively to deny that *corpus ... Domino, et Dominus corpori*—the body is for the LORD, and the LORD for the body.

Fornication is cleaving in the sense of close haptic joining; for Christians, it's also cleaving in the sense of sundering because the flesh that fornicates is flesh already haptically intimate with Jesus, and the intimacies of fornication require separation from Jesus's flesh. The double sense of cleaving, joining and sundering, is vividly present in fornication because in order to fornicate, sundering is necessary so that a new and noncomposible joining can be performed. Christian flesh is already committed, already haptically joined to Jesus's flesh; for any flesh in that condition, meretricious cleaving requires sundering, and the verb shows this with precision. The extent to which Christian flesh fornicates, whether scandalously or idolatrously, is the extent to which it relinquishes its cleaving to Jesus.

3.3   Attention and Hagiography

—Are, then, fornications forbidden to Christian flesh? If they speak against the Jesus-cleaved identity of that flesh, surely, they come under the ban. Sex with temple prostitutes, just like other idolatries, and like adultery and eating food offered to idols, are among those fleshly actions Christians are commanded not to do. Doesn't this place Christian fleshly action under precept, and make learning to act as a Christian should act a simple matter of learning the precepts and abiding by them?

—Not quite. To say that an action speaks against the identity of the one performing it, even to say that it is noncompossible with that identity—that you can't perform both kinds of cleaving at the same time, and that the extent to which you perform the one is the extent to which you relinquish the other—is not the same as placing that action under the ban. Paul, when he turns to the question of forbidden foods in the eighth chapter of the first letter to the Corinthians, begins to show the difference:

> about food as idol offering: we know there's no idol in the world and no god but One. . . . But not everyone knows this. Some, even now, have the habit of eating as if making an idol offering; their conscience is polluted because it is weak. Food, however, doesn't commend us to God; we neither lose if we've eaten it nor gain if we haven't. But take care that this freedom of yours doesn't offend the weak. For if those with weak consciences see you, one who does know [the truth about idols], reclining to eat in an idol temple, they might be moved toward eating as an idol offering. And then, brother, the weak for whom Christ died will come to nothing because of your knowledge. Sinning in this way against your brothers, and wounding their weak consciences, you sin against Christ.

Here is an opposition between those who know (*qui habet scientiam*) the difference between idols and the LORD, and those who don't. The difference is ontological: there are no idols (*nullum idolum est in mundo*), and there is no god other than the LORD (*nullus deus nisi unus*). This entails that food cannot, in the order of being, be an idol offering (*idolothytum*). But in the order of the imagination there are many idols; food can be offered to them, and food can be eaten as if it were such an offering. Those who imagine these possibilities—the weak, the *infirmi*—are badly habituated, "they have the habit (*consuetudo*) of eating as if making an idol offering (*quasi idolothytum manducant*)," and their bad habits further their weakness and make them likely to continue such badly imagined eating if they see others, those who don't imagine idols in these ways, *in idolio recumbens*—reclining to eat in an idol temple. If that happens scandal results, meaning an occasion of sin, a deepening of falsely idolatrous imaginings, for those so influenced. The text therefore bans those in the know from acting in such a way as to create a scandal of that kind. This is an instance of fornicating scandalously, and it does seem, at first blush, that it and its like are placed under the ban.

But this is not the case. To see that it is not, there are two essential points.

First, eating, ingesting food, cannot by itself be an offering to idols, and cannot by itself be an occasion for either distance or intimacy between the LORD and the one who eats: Food *nos non commendat Deo*—doesn't commend us to God; eating and refraining from particular foods is neutral with respect to the identity of Christian flesh. Particular dietary practices speak neither for nor against that identity. Paul makes a similar point in the tenth chapter of the same letter, writing that Christians may eat any food sold in the market and any food offered them when they eat with pagans, and may do so *nihil interrogantes propter conscientiam*—asking no questions because of conscientious doubts about what they may eat—and this because of a radical liberty with respect to matters of dietary rule. If the earth and all that is in it belongs to the LORD (*Domini enim est terra et plenitudo eius*), as the twenty-fourth Psalm says (Paul quotes it in the Corinthian correspondence), then its contents cannot, in principle, be divided into clean and unclean things. And this must go not only for food, but for anything with which human flesh might come into contact.

Second, eating is not typically done alone. It is done in the company of those who imagine idols and imagine the possibility of honoring them by eating, even if they know the difference between idols and the LORD. Even those who do know the difference are not free from idolatrous imaginings: no one is, according to the grammar of Christian thought. And so, even when there are no actual idols to whom the food might have been sacrificed and to whose honor it might be eaten, the act of eating can be provocative of idolatry, in oneself and in others with whom one eats. It can be scandalous, an offence to the conscience of others. When that is the case—when, for example, Christians eat with someone else and are told that what is being served *immolaticium est idolis*—is a burnt offering to idols—then they don't eat if it seems that doing so will scandalize.

Christian freedom with respect to cleaving is, therefore, radical in the order of being. There's nothing, no class or category of things with which fleshly intimacies might be had, cleaving to which speaks against the condition of Christian flesh. But matters are more complicated in the orders of seeming and communication. Certain cleavings may, in particular contexts, turn the imaginations of those who do them and see them done idolwards. Christians who care for the sensibilities of others do not perform such cleavings. Paul, and with him (and because of him) many other Christian thinkers and preachers, often speak of such cleavings as placed under the ban. They use verbs of prohibition in the imperative mood, or, excitably, they sweep such actions aside without exception and without remainder: *absit*, and the like, they say.

In fact, however, whether it is a question of having sex with those dedicated to idols, eating food offered to idols, or dressing in clothes that mark their wearers as idolaters (all these are fleshly actions; they all involve cleaving), there are no bans and no precepts and no commandments. There are only, for Christian flesh, descriptive accounts of kinds of fleshly action that sit well with being Jesus-cleaved, and kinds of fleshly action that speak against it. The LORD, in making it possible for us to be cleaved to Jesus, to be limbs of his flesh, asks nothing in return and, therefore, commands nothing, either. Baptism gives a caress, one that brings those caressed into, inside, the flesh of the one giving the caress. It is the paradigm of fleshly gift, and because of that it asks nothing of those who receive it, except that they do receive it, and as fully as possible. The extent to which they receive it is the extent to which they reciprocate it, returning it with appropriate passion; and the extent to which they reciprocate it is the extent to which they do not perform fleshly actions that speak against it.

The imperatives and subjunctives, the lists of fleshly things-to-be-done and fleshly things-not-to-be-done so widely evident in Scripture and tradition, are, according to this (properly Christian) way of thinking, always capable of transfiguration into the indicative. *Don't have sex with temple prostitutes* and *don't eat food offered to idols* can be rendered, when thinking theologically about what they must mean, as *having sex with temple prostitutes / eating food offered to idols isn't what Christian flesh does*. The extent to which these things are done is the extent to which Christian flesh has forgotten itself and is acting in such a way as to contradict what it is, and thereby diminish itself. And since these forgetfulnesses are never rooted in the order of being, where there are no prostitutes (all foods are clean, all flesh is clean, all clothes are clean), identifying them is always indexed to local habits and local norms. Discernment of which fleshly actions speak against being Jesus-cleaved requires, therefore, thick description of local habits. There are no universal norms binding Christian flesh in these matters; that is what Christian freedom with respect to matters of the flesh means.

If, as the seventy-second Psalm says, it's good to cleave to the LORD (*mihi autem adherere Deo bonum est*), then the right question is: what follows, for the flesh, if it accepts the gift of having been cleaved to the LORD in baptism? And what follows if it doesn't? The answer to the first question is glorification (of the LORD, in the flesh); the answer to the second is fornication (with a prostitute, in the flesh). The task of moral theology is to discriminate the one from the other. That task is prosecuted by descriptive analysis of the extent to which, and the ways in which, particular patterns of action diminish those who perform them by distancing them from the LORD who has cleaved them to Jesus. The prodigal in the fifteenth chapter of Luke's Gospel is the paradigm here: he consumes the substance of his inheritance, which is also his own substance, reducing himself (almost) to nothing, which is to say to a condition in which the only thing possible for him is repentance. The prodigal's self-consumption is an almost pure agent-diminishing action, and while it is only in part a fleshly action, it can serve as an almost perfect icon of how it is that Christian flesh diminishes itself by distancing itself from the one with whom it is cleaved. The prodigal was under no command to remain with his loving father. It would have been better for him if he had, and in not doing so he acted in a way that speaks against his identity as the son of such a father. But the father offered him no punishment because of his transgression, and when he repented gave him at once what had always been his, which is everything, pressed down, shaken together, running over. When Christian flesh acts in accord with what it has become in baptism, then it gets the same: the fleshly blessing. When it does not, it gets what the prodigal also got, which is the fleshly curse, a wandering in the wilderness without hope of home, every caress a wound and every mouthful a poison.

—But may it not yet be that some fornicatory cleavings, whether scandalous or idolatrous (3.2), are banned, barred in principle for Christians, because the creatures with which they are sought and performed can prompt only idolatrous cleavings, without tincture of glory? If there are cleavings like that—and surely there are: Isn't sex between adults and children like that? May not sex paid for and receipted be like that? Couldn't eating human flesh be like that?— surely they should be placed under the ban for Christians? Christians ought to be told that cleavings of that sort are *malum in se*, evil in themselves, and should therefore be renounced by precept and command. And doesn't this insight explain why Scripture, even the texts under discussion here, is so happy to speak in the imperative and the subjunctive about some fleshly cleavings? It seems stretched and precious to read these texts as though they could be interpreted descriptively, translated to the indicative. And denying that any fleshly intimacies are placed under the ban in moral theology runs the risk of lacking moral seriousness.

—Perhaps. It's certainly true that Scripture often seems to place particular actions, even particular fleshly cleavings, under the ban, and therefore to treat them, by implication, as intrinsically evil. Recent Catholic magisterial teaching, too, has often advocated this position with respect to some fleshly cleavings. It's also likely the case that seeking fleshly intimacy with some kinds of creature is impossible without treating them as idols by subsuming them into an idolatrous imaginary. There is, no doubt, catechetical and practical utility in so classifying some kinds of fleshly cleaving. But a deeper theoretical consideration still raises doubts.

Consider an adult seeking to cleave to the flesh of a small child. The child's flesh is good because creaturely; the adult's flesh likewise; the caress, understood as fleshly touch providing the gift of flesh reciprocally to those who share it, likewise. Most Christians and most Jews and most pagans think, it seems, that some fleshly intimacies, some cleavings, between children and adults are good and to be sought without the child's consent. All fleshly intimacies shared between parents and infants are without consent because it belongs to infanthood not to be able to give consent. And yet we, most of us, think these intimacies good. Adult couples bring children into being without their consent, and, generally, we think that good too. The intimacies between adults and children that most legal systems place under the ban aren't of that kind; they are, rather, one or another kind of violence. They're intimacies that wound rather than caress.

Are, then, all woundings, all violent cleavings, to be banned for Christian flesh? There are real difficulties here, but the short answer is no, and for three reasons. The first is that it is difficult to determine what counts as violence and what does not, and without such a determination there can be no clarity about which intimacies are in principle to be banned. The second is that some cleavings, some exchanges of touch, that by all usual criteria are violent (the assassin's death-aimed blow is stopped by force; the child's running into the path of an oncoming vehicle is prevented by force; the quarterback is hurled to the ground by a three-hundred-pound weight moving at speed) aren't obviously at odds with Jesus-cleaved flesh. The presence of violence isn't by itself sufficient to yield the required conclusion. And the third is that there are no fleshly intimacies in a fallen world entirely exempt from violence. Even the most tender caress has the possibility of violence very close to it. The view that there are patterns of fleshly intimacy to be banned in principle to Christian flesh typically ignores this by a Manichaean gesture that identifies some cleavings as pristine and perfect and others as violent and vicious; the former are permitted and encouraged, while the latter are banned and vilified. This is not a defensible position.

The most that can be said when speaking in a theoretical register (different things might properly be said in other registers) is that there are uses of the flesh that, for Christians, typically involve idolatrous fornication. These, when they occur, should be taken as evidence that those doing them have largely forgotten the condition of their flesh as cleaved to Jesus and replaced the flesh of those they're trying to cleave to with an idol of their own making. Certain kinds of fleshly intimacies offered to children by adults come under this head. Thinking of them, and others that might be candidates for the ban, in this way does all the work that moral theology needs to do on the question. It may not do all the work that the preacher, the catechist, or the canon lawyer needs to do.

The remedy for fornicatory cleavings, whether idolatrous or scandalous, is single and simple. It has nothing to do with forbidding them or banning them. It is only a matter of fleshly attention to the incarnate LORD. Christian flesh lives as what it is—Jesus-cleaved—when, and only when, it's attentive to the one to whom it cleaves. When its attention wanders elsewhere, toward the things that are not, fleshly cleavings wander also, and become idolatrous. Caresses are offered to what cannot return them; they then wound the one with whom fleshly commerce is being had, or trail off into the void of self-pleasing, as Jesus is forgotten. When Jesus is remembered, and his caresses received and reciprocated, flesh remembers itself and begins to cease to fornicate. The prohibition and the precept offer only illustrative guidance here; they don't get at fornication's root. Hagiography is more effective: writing the holy, showing how Christian flesh comports itself when attentive to the LORD to whom it cleaves, can show what fornicators need, and thus remember them. Prohibitions produce a striving toward a standard; hagiographies write that standard on the flesh.

Consider, for example, torture as an instance of violent fleshly cleaving. Those attracted to the thought that there is a type of act referred to by the word, and that every token of the type is *malum in se*, typically proceed when writing and talking about torture by defining the type and then offering argumentative analysis intended to show what's wrong with every token. This is a possible approach, but it suffers from the usual conceptual weakness, which is that it turns out to be impossible to specify with clarity sufficient to prevent debate the conditions necessary and sufficient to make an act torturous. And since the power of the position rests largely on its promise to be able to do that—to divide human acts neatly into those that constitute torture and those that don't, and to place the former under the ban—the fact that it can't deliver weakens it significantly. The upshot of that weakness is endless debate both about marginal cases (waterboarding? sleep deprivation? etc.) and about whether what's supposed to be wrong with tokens of the type (objectification of the flesh of the tortured? treating the tortured simply as a means? corruption of the torturer? etc.) in fact applies with equal force to every putative instance. Neither the Church's magisterium, nor the jurists of national and transnational courts, nor the formulators and glossators of transnational conventions governing conduct in time of war have managed to overcome these weaknesses. Striving toward a standard fails exactly to the extent that the standard isn't clear, and in the case of torture it isn't very clear. This isn't to say that forbidding torture by definition and precept is useless; neither is it to say that there are no contexts in which this is the right approach to take. Even for Christians, preachers and catechists might sometimes reasonably take this approach. Certainly, the Church often has. For moral theology, though, the approach is dubious.

Hagiography—writing the holy, showing in words the lineaments of a life suitable to Jesus-cleaved flesh—does better as a stance in moral theology. It is a stance committed to showing what is good and what is not, how the saints act and how they do not, without commitment to the thought that there is a code to which the saints conform, or a demand to which they give their consent. The saintly act, the fleshly life responsive to Jesus, is one best characterized as a matter of the attentive Jesus-cleaved gaze. That gaze, faced with flesh, offers the caress rather than the wound without having to decide exactly where the boundary between the two is drawn. The moral theologian who knows how to use hagiography writes, in the case of torture, a life in which holiness is evident exactly in refusing the demand to inflict systematic violence on the flesh of another for reasons of state; or in which an otherwise holy and exemplary life—for example, that of Thomas More—is shown to be blemished by involvement in the use of such methods. To show, narratively or iconically, what it is like to refuse use of the thumbscrew, the rack, the genital electroshock, or the progressive mutilation of the flesh, even when there are the usual apparently good reasons (protecting the innocent etc.) for doing such things, is hagiographic. Such showings provide clear cases of what saints do and don't do, and they do this without resort to the categories of demand or ban or duty. Hagiographies perform and promote only one thing: attention to Jesus as the gift's giver, and attention to those whose flesh participates in his, whether by baptism's cleaving or by the image given in creation. They show the state of things and the state we're in, and in that way they're formative of those who attend to them.

4 CLOTHES

FLESH IS ORDINARILY CLOTHED, and the wearing of clothes is an intimate fleshly matter. Clothing touches the skin on the inside, and on the outside separates flesh from world. Wearing clothes is tactile first and last, and therefore fundamentally a matter of and for the flesh. Are there meretricious modes of dress for Christians, clothing that speaks against Christian flesh, whether by way of idolatry or scandal? Are there clothes that glorify that flesh, and its LORD to whom it is cleaved? Is there a Christian grammar of thought about clothes, and a Christian habitus with respect to the wearing of them? To answer these questions, clothing needs first to be related to nakedness (4.1), and then to baptism (4.2), in which there is found something like properly Christian clothing. There are clothes for other liturgical occasions, too (4.4), and these have Christian significance. But most clothing is adiaphorous for Christians (4.3), and this is evident and important in the way that Christian flesh approaches the distinguishing of males from females by conventions of dress (4.5), as it also is in its approach to those modes of dress that produce scandal (4.6).

4.1 Clothing and Nakedness

Flesh's porous boundary is its skin. It's by way of skin that flesh contacts bodies and touches other flesh. Ordinarily, human skin is covered, in whole or in part, with something other than itself, something human-made. These coverings are clothes. Clothes need not be next to the skin; they can be layered one over another—the coat that covers the jacket that covers the shirt are all clothes, even if only the shirt is next to the skin. And not everything that covers the skin is clothing. Coverings that immobilize the wearer by providing a carapace (tanning beds; full-body scanners; sleeping bags) fail to be clothes, no matter how close to the skin they may be. Clothes, skin-close, permit their wearers to move through the world even while shielding them from direct contact with that world and from fleshly caresses. Most humans spend most of their waking hours at least partly clothed.

What, more exactly, is clothing for? Four overlapping purposes are easily distinguishable.

First, clothes protect. What they protect against may be independent of human agency. That's usually the case with weather: clothes protect flesh against cold, heat, rain, snow, wind, sun, and so on. Sometimes, too, clothes protect against direct human aggression (bulletproof vests), or dangers produced as side effects of human agency (smog masks). And sometimes they protect the flesh of those doing kinds of work that would otherwise injure flesh (welders' goggles; gardeners' gloves). Clothes, in all these cases, protect the flesh's fragility. Death or injury might be the result of the absence of protective clothing.

Second, clothes enhance fleshly powers: the racing swimmer's suit reduces the drag of her unclothed flesh; the hiker's boots permit walking long distances on rough ground; the hunter's night-vision goggles allow slaughter in the dark. All these count as clothes: they cover some part of the skin while still permitting mobility, and they make it possible for the flesh to do something otherwise impossible or difficult.

Third, clothes badge their wearers: they identify their wearers as being of a kind, serving a function, or participating in a kind of activity. Clothing that protects or enhances may also badge (workers' protective clothes badge them as persons doing that kind of work); but most sartorial badges do not immediately protect the flesh from a threat, or enhance its performance. Rather, they serve to communicate something about their wearers. Priests, vested, consecrate the host and elevate it before the congregation; police, uniformed, make an arrest; doctors, white-coated, probe, palpate, consult, and prescribe. The clothes these people wear, uniforms in these cases, badge them for their work. Uniforms do other things as well—inspire fear or lust or gratitude, for example—but they do at least this.

Sartorial badging also communicates age and sex and status. All human cultures have more or less strongly marked local sartorial indicators for these things, and evident contravention of them (a dhoti-wearing woman in Delhi; a skirt-wearing man in Chicago) typically causes at least tension and sometimes violence. The poor and the rich are also typically badged sartorially, as are the young and the old, and contravention of these local norms, too, often makes what might otherwise be smooth social interactions noticeably more sticky. Panhandling while wearing what look locally like the clothes of the rich, for example, would do this.

Sartorial badging doesn't travel well; what's immediately recognizable as having a particular sartorial meaning in one place may elsewhere communicate nothing but puzzlement, or something contradictory to what its meaning was at home. What sartorial badging communicates is also largely tacit: even those who can read the local badges with ease, precision, and subtlety are unlikely to be able to say what meanings they're giving to the badges they see, even when, as is usually the case, those meanings are rich, permitting complex and friction-free social interactions. Sartorial badges are effective local communicators, but they don't easily lend themselves to removal from the tacit sphere, and that, in large part, is why they don't travel well.

Fourth, clothes are ornaments. They are put on to please those who wear them and to delight or impress or manipulate others. This is clear enough in the case of the ear stud, the necklace, and the ring; but it's also the case when clothes enhance or occlude particular features of the flesh. The heel of a shoe can increase apparent height; the cut of a shirt can decrease apparent girth; the padding of a jacket can emphasize shoulder breadth; the bias of a dress can focus attention on the breasts or the hips.

These four—protection, enhancement, badging, and ornament—are the principal purposes of clothing. There is no clean separation among them. Many sartorial ensembles serve most of these purposes at once: the football player's on-field uniform protects, enhances, badges, and ornaments all at once, as does the office worker's suit and the day laborer's work gear. But some ensembles or particular pieces of clothing serve mostly one or another of these purposes. Few people wear goggles against snow glare because they think they look good in them; and fewer wear filigreed silver earrings for protection of the flesh against damage.

Human flesh may also be naked, unclothed. All human flesh, once it ceases to live symbiotically within the flesh of its mother, enters the world naked—

usually to be clothed by others almost at once. And for most humans past the age of five or so, some clothes are worn during the majority of waking hours. This distinguishes human creatures from almost all (perhaps all) others. But there are always also interludes of nakedness, some embraced willingly (for bathing, for the exchange of caresses, for medical examination and healing, for athletic performance, for comfort, to provide pleasure to a lover or to oneself), some undertaken, willingly or not, as part of a commercial exchange (prostitution, striptease, as an object to be represented in paint or photograph or film), and some forced (the infant's dressings and undressings, the stripping and parading of a victim for humiliation, the undressing of flesh so that it may be tortured, the preparation of an unconscious patient for surgery). Some interludes of nakedness may include all these elements.

Even when flesh returns to body in death, the dialectic of divesting and vesting typically continues: the corpse may be stripped and washed and anointed, then to be reclothed for display or burial or burning. The rhythm of dressing and undressing provides one of the ordering principles of a human life, and it is an extraordinarily complex one. Sartorial rhythms and choices provoke more human ingenuity and take more human energy than almost any others; they are rivalled only by the ingenuity and energy given to gastronomic and sexual rhythms and choices.

If clothes protect, enhance, badge, and ornament flesh, nakedness leaves it unprotected, unenhanced, unbadged, and without ornament—or at least with only those ornaments and badges wrought upon or within its fabric (surgical implants, piercings, tattoos, circumcisions). Nakedness therefore removes most signs of status, most ornamentation, and all protection against ordinary fleshly fragility. It leaves the marks of sex and age, and with them something of the flesh's history—scars, wrinkles, discolorations. Public nakedness exposes what's ordinarily hidden and removes what's ordinarily seen. Solitary nakedness does too, and this explains why some people prefer not to be naked even when alone, or sedulously avoid looking at themselves even when they are naked alone and without need for protection against immediate dangers; but public nakedness adds a level of danger and unease because it makes flesh available to the unpredictable gaze (and perhaps touch) of others, and because it largely removes control over appearance and presentation. This is made worse when public nakedness is involuntary. For an adult to be stripped unwillingly is a kind of torture; unknowingly to be seen naked by others is to be made subject to uninvited gazes. In both cases, control is removed, danger intensified, and embarrassment (in the milder cases) and terror (in the more extreme ones) the likely and proper responses.

There are similar, though much more complex, difficulties with the making of images of nakedness, whether in words, photographs, paintings, or film. Even when consent is given for the making of such images, there's loss of control over the situations in which, and the persons by whom, the images are used. And without consent, if images of nakedness are made without knowledge or under compulsion, then the same difficulties are present, but now added to and exacerbated by ignorance or compulsion.

The dangerous vulnerability of naked flesh also explains why offering it to another can be such a powerful gift. Willingly undressing for someone else is an offer of oneself largely unprotected, unbadged, and unornamented. It ordinarily requires trust that the gift will be received appropriately: without violence, ridicule, or other kinds of blindness to what's being offered. Even if the stripping is done for pay, or with medical attention in mind, or because local habits make it unremarkable in a particular context (beaches in southern Europe; saunas and steam rooms; massage tables; nudist preserves), some modicum of trust is needed. When trust is present, and especially when undressing is reciprocal and two naked bodies of flesh face one another and exchange caresses, a depth of intimacy results that is possible only because nakedness has the protective artifice of clothing as its complement.

4.2 Clothing and Baptism

What difference does flesh becoming Jesus-cleaved in baptism make to the use of clothes, and to the rhythm of divesting and vesting by which most human lives are marked? Is Christian flesh related differently to its own nakedness, and to the nakedness of others, by its Jesus-cleaving?

Christian flesh is ordinarily clothed; nakedness is not its norm. The Jesus-cleaved, like most humans, cleave also to clothes, covering their flesh with silks and leathers and cottons and linens. Mostly, Christian flesh is intimately touched by these things, and there has been, in the long tradition, a marked Christian suspicion of nakedness and a tendency to contrast Christian attitudes to this matter with pagan ones. Pagans, those not formed by explicit knowledge of and response to the LORD, the god of Abraham and Jesus, are more likely to be at ease with nakedness—at the baths, in the bedroom, in the arena, at the beach, outdoors when weather permits—than are Christians; they are more likely, too, to want to represent nakedness—in sculpture, painting, film, photograph, and words—than Christians are. It's rare to find nakedness depicted within the precincts of a Christian church; and rare (though perhaps less than it was) to find Christians among the practitioners and advocates of public nakedness. And there is almost no tradition, among Christians, of representing the natal or resurrected flesh of Jesus unclothed. The exceptions (and even in these cases his flesh is rarely shown completely naked) are, significantly, mostly found in representations of Jesus's baptism, death on the cross, and taking down therefrom for burial.

Baptism shows something important about the relation of nakedness to Christian flesh. It's the rite that both shows and effects the cleaving of pagan (or Jewish) flesh to the flesh of Jesus, and nakedness is proper to it. That is, baptizands ideally undergo their baptisms naked in order to show that they are being baptized as flesh, in the flesh, and that it is exactly their flesh that is transfigured by being cleaved to Jesus. Naked pagan flesh (a different account is needed for the baptisms of Jews) descends into the chaos-waters of the baptismal font; the LORD moves upon the surface of those waters as the triune name is invoked, in recapitulation of the LORD's movement upon the waters in creation; pagan flesh is transfigured in those waters by cleaving to Jesus; and when it ascends from the waters, in recapitulation of its birth from its mother, it is at once clothed in a white baptismal garment, which is an actual piece of clothing worn next to the skin, as well as an element of the sacrament by means of which the newly baptized's cleansing from sin and cleaving to Jesus is shown and effected. The rhythm of the rite moves from undressing (the removal of clothes from pagan flesh) to redressing (the putting on of the baptismal garment).

Most Christian baptisms, now, don't require, and most don't involve, the nakedness of those being baptized. When a baptizand is naked it's almost always an infant. Christians are uneasy about nakedness, especially the nakedness of adults, even in baptism. But something is lost by that uneasiness. Clothed baptizands are still baptized, still washed from sin, still cleaved to Jesus. The efficacy of the rite does not depend on nakedness. But the nakedness of baptizands, together with their subsequent dressing, shows and participates in what's happening to them with a clarity and force that is seriously obstructed by clothing. Pagan natal flesh's coming to be is necessarily without clothes; Christian natal flesh's cleaving to Jesus is obscured by them, even if not made impossible.

This difference is because Christian flesh comes into being by way of the transfiguration of already existing pagan or Jewish flesh, while pagan natal flesh comes into being where, before, there was only sperm and egg, separate and seeking to join. Baptism, which brings Jesus-cleaved flesh into being, does not do so by destroying the pagan flesh on which it works. The LORD does not proceed by erasure: Abram isn't destroyed and replaced by Abraham, and neither is Saul by Paul; the natal flesh of Jesus is not destroyed by death and then replaced by new flesh in his resurrection, but (with the prolepsis of the transfiguration in mind, 2.3) transfigured into it. The same is true of the relation between pagan natal flesh and baptized flesh. There is, nonetheless, a profound change. Baptized flesh's cleavings are fundamentally different from those of natal flesh, and this difference is occluded by baptizing clothed flesh. When that is done, when the baptizand is clothed, the transfigured flesh, now cleaved to Jesus, typically retires from the ecclesial scene to a private place, there either to disrobe and put on the white baptismal garment marking its transfiguration or, worse, to put the baptismal garment on over the clothes worn before and during baptism. In both cases, the scene is changed and the other members of the body that the baptizand has now joined are left behind. When clothes are changed, the act of doing so speaks strongly against—misrepresents—what has just taken place: something (the pagan flesh's clothes) has not been transfigured by the baptismal bath, and must therefore be removed before the new clothes can be put on. The work of baptism is, in this scenario, completed extra-baptismally. And if the baptismal garment is put on over the pagan clothes, then something interposes between transfigured flesh and the flesh of Christ to which it has been cleaved by baptism. In these ways, clothed baptisms occlude or contradict what's happening. That is not to say that such baptisms fail as baptisms. Their validity and efficacy is given by the use of water and the triune name. But it is to say that the form of the rite when the baptizand is clothed speaks against what the rite accomplishes.

Baptism suggests nakedness as a prelude to Jesus-cleaving; and once flesh is so cleaved, its clothing in a white garment shows what happens to it. Those clothes are used again when Christian flesh returns to body in death: it belongs properly and ideally to the funerary rite to drape the casket or the body or both in white as reminder of what the flesh that died and became body was, and to underscore the hope of what it will be again, at the resurrection. These white garments are the paradigmatic Christian clothing, and their use is restricted to the beginning of the Christian life and the transitus between this life and that of the world to come.

These white garments are the only fully and properly Christian clothes. If there is a Christian uniform, this is it. It's a peculiar one. It's meant to be worn only at the beginning of the Christian life here below, in baptism; and at its end, in burial. After death, Christian flesh has no need of clothes: in the resurrection there are none, as there also weren't in the garden before the Fall. None of the purposes served by clothes have purchase in heaven, and this is especially true of the purpose served by the white garment. All resurrected heavenly flesh is beyond possibility of sin, and therefore also beyond need for sartorial marking of sinlessness. The Christian uniform is therefore temporary and occasional. It badges, as clothes often do; but not for the world. The white garment finds its place only within the Church, among those likewise Jesus-cleaved; it sends no message to the pagans. Once the white garment has been put off, Christian flesh is, and ought to be, save for some exceptions for scandal (4.6), sartorially indistinguishable from pagan flesh. Local sartorial conventions, whatever they are, are wholly adoptable by Christian flesh; and where there are Christian uniforms worn for badging or protection in the pagan world, a sartorial mistake has been made.

4.3 Clothing and Convention

In the world of the trope, clothes—their putting on and taking off—are of considerable importance in the Christian tradition. The Christian, for example, is said to be one who puts on and wears Jesus, whether at baptism or more generally, and so, by only a small extension of thought, one who can properly be said to wear Jesus, to wear the LORD as a garment. In the third chapter of his letter to the Galatians, Paul writes, *quicumque enim in Christum baptizati estis Christum induistis*—whoever's baptized in Christ has put on Christ. He writes immediately after this that in Christ there's no Jew or Greek, no slave or free person, and no man and woman. All these are one in Christ, and that can be expressed by saying that all are identically clothed with Jesus. Christians wear Jesus like a garment because, or just as, they are cleaved to him. Both tropes (cleaving and wearing) suggest fleshly intimacy: clothes are next to the skin, typically, and cleaving is a metaphor of union (3.1). But these tropes have nothing directly to do with actual clothes, and the relevance they have to those is indirect.

The depictions of Adam's and Eve's nakedness and clothing in the garden are more direct, and perhaps more productive for thinking about Christian clothes. At the end of the second chapter of Genesis, after Adam, The Man, has named the animals and failed to find among them any who might remedy his solitude (*non est bonum esse hominem solum*), and after the LORD has made Eve, The Woman, for The Man exactly as that remedy, "they—Adam and Eve— were naked (*nudi*) and didn't blush (*non erubescebant*)." Shortly, they eat the forbidden fruit, come to see that they are indeed naked (*cumque cognovissent esse se nudes*), and at once make aprons (*perizomata*) from the leaves of the fig tree—coverings for at least their genitals, which have now become *pudenda*, things to be ashamed of. Their eyes have been opened, and they can now see something they didn't see before they ate. What they see is that their flesh is naked, and it is this seeing that causes blushes: they are now differently related to and differently perceptive of what their flesh is and how it might be impli- cated with the flesh of others.

The LORD discovers what has happened and curses, variously, Adam, Eve, and the serpent, and then, "the LORD God made garments of skin (*tunicas pelliceas*) for Adam and Eve, and put them on them (*induit eos*)." The verb for the putting on of clothes is the same here as the one used in Galatians. No fur- ther mention is made of the fig-leaf aprons, nor of the garments of skin. The couple go from being naked and unashamed to being doubly clothed, once by themselves, out of shame, and once by the LORD, perhaps as punishment, or at least as a mark of their new condition. The context certainly suggests something like this: the leather garments are made and given immediately after the curses.

This story is full of clothes, and of interpretive possibility. The commenta- tors, Jewish and Christian, have not held back. Some structural features of the account, reproduced and elaborated by many of the commentators, are clear enough, and suggestive for the question about vesting and divesting Christian flesh. One, fundamental, is that nakedness, the flesh uncovered by clothes, be- longs to the order of creation. Adam and Eve, as they were made and before their fall, were not clothed, and not only were they not abashed by this state of things, but the LORD, their maker, took it to be *valde bonum*, very good, as good as it could be. It's common for commentators to suggest that *nudus* doesn't mean only or merely the absence of garments, but rather the clothing of the flesh in light as a sign of its unimpaired intimacy with its maker and, correspondingly, of its status as very good, and even blessed. But even if this line is followed, the clothing affirmed of prelapsarian human flesh is metaphorical. Eve and Adam, until the fig leaves, are without coverings made by human hands, and it's only coverings of that kind that count as nonmetaphorical clothes. Even the leather garments aren't clothes, properly speaking, because they're made and given by the LORD. That the garments of skin are unusual in this sense—unusual exactly in not being clothes—is recognized by the majority of commentators, Jewish and Christian, who understand them to be the garments of mortality—skin as representative of flesh tending toward body—and the LORD's gift of them to Adam and Eve (and all of us) as the promised gift of death. This reading makes it possible to say that the LORD's promise of death to the couple if they eat the forbidden fruit, a promise denied by the serpent, is fulfilled, in the sense that they become mortal rather than that they at once fall dead. The reading even makes it possible to gloss a feature of the Latin text, which reads, in the case of both promise and denial, *morte morieris*, literally, "you will die with death," by saying that the death of which they'll die (*mors-morte*) is mortality, and that the future tense of the verb (*morior-morieris*) indicates exactly that they won't die yet but, rather, have now become mortal. Their garments of skin, then, are their own skin, now mortal. This is one more instance of clothing as trope, rather than clothing as actual clothes.

It's possible also to read the text as being about actual clothes, actual leather tunics made by the LORD as gift and protection for those about to be expelled from Eden into a world where they'll need all the protection they can get. There are some useful avenues of thought suggested by this reading, but it is less capable of accounting for the particulars of the text in which it's found—specifically the *morte morieris* phrase—and gives less credit to the difference between garments made by the LORD and garments made by humans, the latter being clothes properly speaking.

One purpose of clothing for Christians, the Genesis story may suggest, is to remedy shame—literally, in the story's language, to spare blushes. For humans, and perhaps especially for men and women, to be naked in one another's sight, this suggests, is an occasion for shame that clothing can protect against. Baptism reverses this. Fallen and shameful flesh is drowned in that bath, and the clothing it needs when it emerges isn't a remedy for shame—what is there about human flesh cleaved to Jesus's flesh, human flesh now wearing Jesus, that could produce shame?—but instead a celebration of rebirth and an anticipation of final resurrection. Christian naked flesh, in this reading, is now once again *valde bonum*, very good, and neither the relations between the sexes nor anything else requires clothing. Nakedness glorifies the LORD, and protective clothes are meretricious. Concordant with this line of thinking is the speculation that Christian resurrected flesh, heavenly flesh, will necessarily be naked.

Its garments of skin will have been taken from it—certainly so, if these are understood to represent mortality—and its fig leaves, along with all other artifacts, will be no more. Flesh then will once again be clothed in light, which is another way of saying naked (and radiant), though the garments of light it will then receive are immeasurably better than those with which Adam and Eve were clothed before the Fall, and that is because they are an element of the world's heavenly fulfilment, which is—it is axiomatic for Christian thought to say—an improvement upon the unfallen state of things in Eden.

—But does this mean that Christians are fornicating, acting meretriciously, whether idolatrously or scandalously, whenever they wear clothes now, after baptism but before the general resurrection? Does it mean that Christian flesh not only doesn't need clothes, but performatively contradicts what it is, what it has become in baptism, when it covers itself with them? Should Christians now go naked as a matter of course?

—No. Christians aren't gymnosophists, even though the thought that they should be has occasionally surfaced within the tradition, and for something like the pattern of reasoning just sketched. What it does mean is that Christians have been liberated from the tyranny of clothes. Clothes, for them, are, like language and food, necessities for a while (as there won't be clothes in heaven, so also there won't be language or food), but necessities whose local norms bear approximately the same relation to Christian flesh as the norms of particular local languages bear to the word of the LORD given in the canon of Scripture. The relation in question is one of conventional necessity: Christian flesh must be covered, the LORD's word must be spoken, clothes are necessary for the one and languages for the other, both clothes and languages are locally normed, and so Christians adopt the sartorial and linguistic norms of the places in which they find themselves while recognizing that those norms have, and can have, no more than local purchase. They have, and can have, nothing essential to do with the fabric of the Christian life. That women wear skirts is a local fact like in kind to the fact that the French language genders its nouns. If Christians live where women wear skirts or where French is what's spoken, then Christian women will wear skirts and speak French. They won't, however, or oughtn't, think that wearing skirts has anything to do with the fact that their flesh is Christian, Jesus-cleaved, any more than they will, or ought to, think that their gendering of nouns has anything to do with the word of the LORD.

This position removes burdens. Those who hold it are freed from the thought that any mode of dress can, *ipso facto*, simply by its form, speak against, or for, the fact of Christian flesh. A woman might wear pants as well as skirts; a man might wear skirts as well as pants; either might wear anything local norms prescribe for the other, and yet be as well situated with respect to the Jesus-cleaved nature of their flesh as if they abided by local norms on these matters. There's freedom in the reverse direction as well: local norms about clothing, again in this just like local norms about speech and writing, are often gorgeously complex. The French subjunctive and the difference between a single-vented and a double-vented jacket are phenomena with their own peculiar beauty. Christians who see that these things are what they are—local beauties—can embrace them as such without idolatry and become connoisseurs of clothes or of speech without contravening who they are.

There's a further implication. It is that clothing itself, any covering of the flesh, has, with baptism, lost its deep necessity. It's on the way to abolition, and so there can be nothing in principle against nakedness for Christians. Christian flesh has, ideally, no shame, just as Christian life is, ideally, free from fear, and so when nakedness offers itself as a local norm (in the sauna, at the beach, with the beloved) Christians have no reasons to refuse it other than whatever local ones are in play. There is, in brief, no specifically Christian habit of clothing or nakedness, in just the same way that there is no specifically Christian habit of language. These things are all, for Christians, adiaphorous: Paul's motto, *omnia mihi licent*, applies to modes of dress (and nakedness) as much as to modes of eating and drinking, and that's why, typically, what Christian flesh does about clothes is just what the locals do, whatever that is. But Paul also writes *sed non omnia expediunt*—but not everything's useful or appropriate, and that motto, too, can find application here, and in so doing provide some exceptions to the general principle that clothes (and nakedness) are adiaphorous for Christians.

4.4 Liturgical Clothes

The first exception has to do with badging, other than the fundamental and transient badge of the baptismal white garment. Christianity has been prolific in attending to and producing sartorial badges of states and habits of life. This is most especially true of the priestly state, which is deeply sartorially marked for both Jews and Christians. But it is true also of other states: diaconal, episcopal, and vowed, whether as religious or as married. The sartorial marking of baptism has already been noted. It's true, too, of some particular functions and associations, even when these are not themselves states of life. The Knights of Columbus are sartorially marked in these ways, as are, for example, many of the sodalities and confraternities dedicated to the Blessed Virgin. The scapular is among the more common items of clothing used for such marking. Many Christians, therefore, both are and want to be marked sartorially as Jesus-cleaved; these badgings may extend to the indication of particular functions within the community or the world and of particular, specialized, habits of relating to the LORD.

For example: in the twenty-eighth chapter of Exodus a detailed description is given of the clothes to be made for Aaron and his brothers. These are priestly clothes, clothes for *sacerdotes*, and, the text says, *faciesque vestes sanctas Aaron fratri tuo in gloriam et decorem*—you shall make holy clothes for Aaron, your brother, for glory and for beauty. The prescription that follows is precise and exhaustive, and it uses again the expression "for glory and for beauty." The clothes of the Aaronic priesthood make those who wear them glorious and beautiful, not because of properties intrinsic to the clothes (the clothes are nothing but thread and fabric and dye and polished metal, however gorgeous), but because the clothes badge them by the LORD's command as set apart for a peculiar intimacy with the LORD and a peculiar work for the community of the elect. The clothing of the Christian priesthood is the same: it glorifies and beautifies those who wear it, and by doing this marks them for the peculiar work of preaching the word and celebrating the sacraments. Vestments are to priestly flesh—flesh sacramentally set apart for priestly work—in one important respect as the white baptismal garment is to baptized flesh: that is, the clothes in both cases show and participate in the condition of those clothed in it, in the one case that of being Jesus-cleaved, and in the other that of standing as Jesus to the people, which itself requires being Jesus-cleaved. Priestly and baptismal garments are unlike in many other ways, not least in the fact that the former are put on and off frequently, whereas the latter are put on and off only once, at baptism, not to be put on again until death.

It isn't that priestly vestments or baptismal garments make those who wear them saintly. They don't remove the possibility of sin for the baptized; and they don't make priests, even while they're doing what priests do, incapable of deep, even mortal, sin. The same, *mutatis mutandis*, applies to baptismal garments. But what priestly garments do, in addition to badging and participating in the sacramental tranformation of the flesh of those who wear them, is adorn their wearers for the LORD, make them beautiful for the LORD's kiss and embrace.

Clothes adorn ordinarily, by local convention and for local purposes; those adornments are adiaphorous for Christian flesh—to be indulged in or not, as local norms and particular needs dictate. But these baptismal and priestly adornments are not adiaphorous because they are gifts returned to the LORD who prescribes them, gifts that, when returned, make the returner beautiful and glorious, as the text from Exodus specifically says. The LORD's embrace of the baptized is in part prepared for and returned sartorially; similarly for the LORD's embrace of the priest. Sartorial badging for office in this gift-return sense isn't required for Christians (*omnia mihi licent*, after all), but its principled and complete rejection would not be appropriate (*non omnia expediunt*).

4.5   Male and Female Clothes

The second exception to the general claim that clothes (and nakedness) are adiaphorous for Christians is shown in aphoristic form by the texts already mentioned from the third chapter of Galatians.

> Whoever's been baptized in Christ has put on Christ (*Christum induistis*): there's neither Jew nor Greek, neither slave nor free, not male and female, for all of you are one in Christ Jesus (*omnes enim vos unus estis in Christo Iesu*).

The connection of thought is important here. It's because the baptized have put on Jesus and, therefore, have become cleaved to him, that they're all one—and this oneness is specified by the denial of the matched pairs Jew/Greek, slave/free, male/female. These matched pairs are not in every respect the same. The Jew/Greek and slave/free pairs are, in the text, negated in neither/nor form, while the male/female pair is negated in not/and form. This is in part because Paul here echoes the text of Genesis ("male and female he created them"), but it also shows that the male/female pair is rooted in creation as the slave/free and Jew/Greek dichotomies are not. However they're construed, though, oneness removes the dualities in the (metaphorical) sense that Christians aren't clothed with them, haven't put them on (*induere*), in any final or deep sense. Christians are, finally and deeply, clothed with Jesus, and that clothing overcomes—puts off—any and all other clothes. The text is not best read to mean that there are, after baptism, no Christian males and no Christian females, no Christian Jews and no Christian pagans (a gloss on "Greek"), and no Christian slaves or nonslaves. The male-female distinction continues within the Church, without abolition, and even, most Christian thinkers have speculatively concluded, into the general resurrection (Augustine is decisive on this for the Latin-using West, and rightly so)—and this is true even if it's difficult to find a compelling specification of what, exactly, constitutes the difference between men and women (fleshly form? chromosomes? genes? procreative functions?—none of these will quite do). The Jew-pagan distinction also continues within the Church in the sense that Jews can be, and are, cleaved to Christ by baptism, just as non-Jews can and are, and that the difference between Jews and pagans isn't abolished by baptism, even if it is transfigured by it. The slave-free distinction is different: slavery indicates a local and contingent relation, and the Church has come to see what Paul did not, which is that it can and should be abolished prior to the end, and need not, therefore, continue to mark the Church's body in the same way that the other distinctions do. The male/female and Jew/Greek distinctions remain, then, but now transfigured. Those whose flesh is Jesus-cleaved are distinguished in the ways indicated by those matched pairs only in a preliminary way. The distinctions do not go all the way down: the only (metaphorical) clothing that does is Jesus. Those clothes can't be put off, and they provide a unity deeper than any distinction, sartorial or other.

What, then, for example, about local sartorial norms that distinguish male from female? These often present themselves as, first, not to be transgressed on pain of exclusion or violence; and, second, as entailed by and inseparable from the physical (and sometimes intellectual) natures of men and women. When those two families of justification for gender-specific sartorial norms are intertwined, transgression of such norms tends to be seen as transgression of an order of nature, and those who transgress as properly punishable for doing so. These are, from a Christian point of view, pagan patterns of reasoning. Jesus has overturned them, and those who have cleaved to him and are clothed with him are no longer subject to them, even when they abide by them. When Christians do abide by sartorial norms that distinguish men from women, they do so, ideally if not always actually, as if they were what they actually are, which is local conventions with local utility.

However, when such norms present themselves as something more than that, and when they seem so to be taken by most who observe them locally, then Christians may judge that abiding by them as the locals do is not simply adiaphorous. To observe local norms in this matter in such a way as to make Christian dress indistinguishable from local pagan dress would be, or might be, to support a pagan view that speaks against being Jesus-cleaved. Dressing as a man, or as a woman, in such a way that the reframing of such dressing by Jesus is ignored typically moves those who do it in the direction of, first, thinking that there is something Christian about such norms; and then, second, toward active support of pagan modes of thinking about those norms as intimate with the natures of men and women and reflective of the order of being. Much better—more coherent with being Jesus-cleaved—would be to adopt styles of dress that signal the subordination of sartorial gender marking to sartorial gender transfiguration. This could be done by mixing local norms: men could adopt some of the sartorial marks taken locally to be proper to women, and the other way around. In the early twenty-first century in North America, this might mean that men sometimes paint their nails and wear skirts, while women sometimes stop shaving their legs and wear neckties. A simple switchover, where men consistently adopt women's local sartorial norms and women men's, wouldn't bring about the desired result, which is to remind Christians of what local sartorial norms are (pure conventions) and to signal to pagans something of what it means to cleave to Jesus. A simple switchover would be as likely to signal a reversed male-female identitarianism as an undercutting of just that identitarianism. Fluid mixing does better, sits closer to the effect that Jesus-cleaving has on male and female flesh, which is to subordinate its gender identity to its cleaving to Jesus and, thus, to liberate it from hard-identitarian sartorial norms on these matters.

This second exception to the generally adiaphorous character of local sartorial norms for Christians is indexical. That is, it's a response to local situations in which sartorial norms for gender badging have become hardened and enforced by violence against or social exclusion of offenders. Not all local situations are like this, though it seems probable that most are. When Christians come to see that their locale is like this, then observing local sartorial norms without transgressive gestures (not necessarily dramatic ones) is to begin, in dress, to speak against the Jesus-cleaving of one's flesh. Christians have often engaged in sartorial transgressions of local gender-marking norms. Most of their sartorial badges, especially those that show priestly office, but also those that show membership in religious orders, have exactly this effect: they desex those who wear them, and stand at odds with local sartorial gender badges. A male priest, when vested, is feminized (this is a traditional Protestant criticism of Catholicism; it should be embraced as accurate and as a good); and a female one masculinized (Protestant priests and ministers sometimes observe this, whether positively or critically; it, too, should be embraced as a good). And the habits of religious orders, arguably, do the same: women who dress in them are desexed, as are men. This is true even when particular offices or memberships are restricted to one sex or the other.

Catholics are tempted, when thinking about and providing norms for the clothing of religious, by the thought that clothes marking gender difference have a deeper significance than they actually do. When Catholics yield to such temptations, they're likely to specify dramatically different sartorial norms for male and female religious. The extent to which that is done is the extent to which the Christian imagination has failed, and there's been a move toward scandalous sartorial fornication—scandalous in the sense that a local sartorial norm has been adopted without permitting it to be transfigured by Jesus. It can hardly be a defense that local norms require sartorial gender differentiation, and that the work of the orders would be hampered if such clothes were not required. Religious orders already contravene local norms ordering procreation, property ownership and transfer, cohabitation, and so on, deeply and dramatically; sartorial contravention would do no more than add one. If male and female religious were indistinguishably dressed within their particular orders, this would be a powerful, and possible, signal of what being Jesus-cleaved does to clothes.

This Catholic failure is an instance of a more general Christian temptation to ignore the fact that local sartorial norms, whether prompted by sexual difference or by other things, are transfigured by Jesus. Christians are tempted even to the point of shunning or otherwise punishing those who don't abide by local sartorial norms: the transvestite may be ostracized or refused participation in the Church's sacramental life; the boy or girl who exhibits sartorial tastes and proclivities locally taken to be more appropriate to the other sex may be disciplined out of them in the name of Christianity. But in fact, Christians are liberated from sartorial markings of a hard identitarian kind, and such disciplinings, punishments, shamings, and shunnings are outflows of a mistaken construal of the grammar of the faith with respect to these questions. Dressing as though to support hard-identitarian norms comes, for Christian flesh, under the Pauline heading of what's neither useful nor appropriate (*non expedire*), while dressing in such a way as to destabilize such norms is permitted (*omnia mihi licent*).

—Surely, though, there are scriptural and deeply traditional sartorial norms, some of them gender marked, prescribed for Christians. Paul seems to say that, for example, women should cover their heads in church; the Jewish community out of which Christianity came was then, and is now in its Orthodox forms, strongly committed to sartorial gender marking; and there is much in the doctrine and discipline of particular churches, including the Catholic Church, that shows commitment to the nonnegotiability and non-fluidity of sartorial gender marking.

—Yes. All that is correct. The line or argument given here would result, if taken seriously, in developments in church discipline, at least. It's offered as a speculation, without commitment as to whether it'll be taken up. But it's not offered without roots in the tradition. The lines of thought sketched here plumb the depths of Christianity; gender-marked sartorial prescriptions and proscriptions belong to the shallows, as is evident from their comparatively undeveloped doctrinal basis.

—Maybe. But even if the sartorial question is like this, it can hardly be claimed that the male-female difference is. That goes deep, is rooted in the creation accounts, and is reflected in the evident morphological, chromosomal, and genetic differences between males and females. The Catholic Church, especially in the magisterial teachings of recent popes (John Paul, Benedict, Francis), appears committed to some version of male-female complementarity. Why shouldn't these differences and complementarities find a representation in different habits of dress for men and women?

—They may. No ban on such differences is suggested here. All that's suggested is that attending to the nature of Christian flesh as Jesus-cleaved shows a fleshly unity that undergirds and overcomes male-female differences, fleshly and other; it also shows that sartorial norms marking gender can have no more than local and conventional meaning for Christians. That's not to say that such norms have no meaning. They can be embraced and found delightful by Christians like any other local beauties; they're an element in the habitus of every human society. But when they're overinterpreted, rooted in the order of things, and sanctioned by violence, Christian flesh shows what it is by sitting loose to them. It already does that by refusing sartorial gender marking in the rite of baptism, and by acknowledging that the life of the world to come to which we look forward, while still containing male and female flesh, won't mark that difference sartorially.

4.6 Scandalous Clothes

Particular sartorial ensembles and conventions are adiaphorous for Christians, except for baptismal garments (4.2) and other liturgical clothes (4.4), which properly, though temporarily and occasionally, belong to Christian flesh. Those are positive exceptions to the general rule. A negative exception is observance of too-rigid sartorial markings of gender (4.5), which can produce scandal by appearing to endorse misprisions of what clothes are and are for. There are other exceptions to the general rule of like kind: occasions, that is, when Christian conformity to sartorial convention might be scandalous in the same way that, following Paul's description, eating food sacrificed to idols might be (5.6). These are cases in which the extent to which Christian flesh is dressed in such a way as to encourage the imagination, whether in the one so dressed or in others seeing it so dressed, that it is an idol offering, an *idolothytum*, is the extent to which it repudiates its condition as Jesus-cleaved and should itself be repudiated. Those who dress themselves in this way are like those who recline in the idol temple to eat: whether or not their own imaginations are directed idol-ward by their clothes, those of others might be, and it would be better for themselves and others that they dress differently.

The principle is clear enough. Its applications are more difficult because considerable understanding of local context is needed before a particular sartorial ensemble can be judged as an idol offering (the same is true for discerning when food might so be taken, 5.6). But some instances are clear enough: the manacles and shackles clothing the flesh of slaves on an auction block to stage them for sale as chattel turn the imaginations of all participants in the scenario, even those of the slaves, idol-wards just to the extent that they understand the arrangements they're participating in. The ornaments and garments that clothe prostitutes' flesh in a brothel to stage them for temporary sexual purposes do the same. Dressing flesh in a uniform that badges its wearers as emissaries of a régime dedicated to slaughter does the same. And dressing in an ensemble whose very existence requires sweatshop labor does the same. This is not an exhaustive list, even for here and now. Many other instances could be offered for other times and places.

These examples share with Paul's treatment of food offered to idols the feature that there's nothing about the clothing—the manacles, the diaphanous robes, the epaulettes, the cheap chain-store pants—considered simply as clothing that makes it an idol offering in the order of being. No clothing can be, *simpliciter*, an idol offering, which is among the reasons that there is, with the exceptions noted, no properly Christian clothing and no Christian reason to renounce or adopt any sartorial ensemble. What makes these clothes such that they can move the imagination idol-wards is, first, a particular set of institutional arrangements (the slave market, the brothel, the fascist army, the sweatshop), and second, the understanding on the part of those who clothe themselves in these ways, and on the part of those who see them so clothed, of the nature of the institutional arrangements in which these clothes participate. Without such understandings, there is no movement of the imagination idol-wards, as is easy to see by imagining these sartorial ensembles represented in fiction (no one thinks the shackled actor a slave), or shown to someone ignorant of the institutional arrangements that give them meaning. But to the extent that there is understanding of those arrangements, and of the clothes that those who inhabit them wear, there is sartorial scandal. Such offerings speak against the Jesus-cleaved nature of the flesh that wears them.

Christian nakedness should be analyzed in the same way. Nakedness by itself never speaks against Christian flesh. It cannot, because the gaze at nakedness—the newly opened eye—that made Eve and Adam blush is not a Christian gaze. When Christians see naked flesh, whether that of the Jesus-cleaved or that of Jews or of pagans, they see flesh already or proleptically cleaved to Jesus. Flesh of that sort can be nothing but beautiful. There's nothing about its exposure to the gaze that could make Christian flesh blush. All nakedness, like all clothes and all food, is not only permitted but delightful for Christian flesh; there is and can be nothing intrinsically wrong with it, as is evident from the nakedness of the baptismal bath which anticipates the nakedness of resurrected flesh. There is in principle no reason for Christian norms and practices about nakedness to differ from local pagan norms. When it's usual in some locale for men and women, whether alone, separately, or together, to be naked, Christians have, in principle, no reason to behave otherwise.

But, as with clothing, there can be situations in which nakedness does speak against Christian flesh, situations in which being naked doesn't glorify the LORD, but rather fornicates scandalously. Nakedness, too, can move the imagination idol-wards. When people are stripped naked against their will, when nakedness is an item in a commercial transaction, when nakedness is used as an instrument to manipulate and control others, when nakedness is an object of the concealed gaze—in all cases of that kind, cases in which nakedness is implicated in a pattern of practice or an institutional form in which it moves the imagination idol-wards, nakedness speaks against Christian flesh by speaking against what it is to be Jesus-cleaved.

A similar pattern of thought can be applied to the more difficult matter of the visual representation and display of nakedness. Making images of the naked flesh of an actual person, whether by drawing, painting, photography, or film, is, by itself, unproblematic for Christian flesh. What could be wrong with making an image of such flesh, Jesus-cleaved and beautiful as it is? Christian judgments that there is something wrong with making such images (and with permitting one's own flesh to be imaged) are almost always articulated with the thought that there's something wrong in principle with image making, a thought that has roots in the scriptural and traditional prohibitions against making images of the LORD. Those prohibitions, however, aren't easy (for Christians) to extend to a ban on image making in general; and when this has been tried, as it was in the iconoclastic controversies of the seventh and eighth centuries, and in the Protestant Reformation of the sixteenth, it has always yielded theological conclusions and ecclesial practices at odds with fundamental Christian convictions, most especially those that have to do exactly with the LORD's incarnation (enfleshment). The long tradition has been prolific in making images of Jesus, Mary, and the saints, and these images, whether in the form of icons taken sacramentally to participate in the LORD's being, or in the more diffuse sense of images usable devotionally or instructionally, have entered deeply into the life of the Church.

These images are, however, only rarely of completely naked flesh. Some approach this (Jesus on the cross; Sebastian *in extremis*), but most are well covered, with special attention to the sexual characteristics—the only significant exception here is images of Mary's naked breasts being sucked by the infant Jesus, which at some periods have been an ecclesial commonplace and at others altogether absent. There is, then, a Christian wariness about liturgical or devotional use of images of unclothed flesh, and a corresponding wariness about the activity of making such images, and of permitting the flesh of actual persons to be used as models for them. That wariness continues into the present.

Why? Two patterns of thought are evident in Christian writing about making images of naked flesh and using such images. One is reasonable and entirely in accord with Christian premises; the other very much less so. The first is a realization that images of naked flesh often are idol offerings in the sense already discriminated. They easily participate in an economy of fleshly idol offerings (Aphrodite might be among the idols to whom such offerings are made; but darker and more violent gods are also possible recipients, including the voracious and violent market in pornography) and, when actual naked flesh models for the image, can place the person whose flesh is imaged into that economy exactly as an idol offering. Those whose flesh is Jesus-cleaved speak against their own flesh when they participate in such an economy, or when they inflame the imaginations of others idol-wards. This objection is reasonable. It participates in the patterns of reasoning about clothes already set out. Less reasonable, though perhaps equally widespread among Christians, is the thought that images of naked flesh are ipso facto offerings to idols. When this pattern of thought is in play it tends to lead to a generic condemnation of such images without attention to the economy to which they belong, as though they could be understood in abstraction from any such economy. This is not reasonable. Anything, including naked flesh, can in principle be imaged by Christians; that, again, is a result of the Jesus-cleaving that happens to flesh in baptism.

Christian flesh can be clothed for protection, enhancement, badging, and ornament without thereby speaking against its identity as Jesus-cleaved. It can also be naked without doing so, whether alone or in public. How Christian flesh dresses, and how often and where it is naked, are at bottom adiaphorous. Christian habits on these matters are largely given by local habits, themselves tremendously varied, which is as it should be. There is no distinctive Christian dress, and no distinctive Christian attitude to clothes or nakedness. The only exceptions are: the need to badge and ornament Christian flesh sartorially to mark and effect its initial cleaving to Jesus; the need to ornament it, occasionally, for particular intimacies with the LORD; the need to resist locally hardened and violent sartorial norms by destabilizing them; and the need to avoid dressing (or being naked) as a form of offering to idols. Abiding by local sartorial norms when they've become hardened, and moving imaginations idolward by dress or nakedness—these are fornicatory uses of clothes that speak against Christian flesh's Jesus-cleaved-ness. Other uses glorify the LORD by appropriately dressing the flesh.

It won't always be easy to tell when a sartorial ensemble is fornicatory. That's because no such ensemble is so in itself, and because knowledge of the context that makes it so isn't equally or easily available to everyone, and can be interpreted differently even when it is available. Christians disagree, therefore, often reasonably, about what constitutes sartorial fornication, and also disagree, and reasonably, about what constitutes sartorial glorification. They should not disagree, however, about the pattern of thought to be used in addressing such questions.

That sartorial ensembles can properly be characterized as idol offerings, and as complicit with rigid and violent local norms, might be taken to provide a set of dress rules for Christians: a tightly corseted set of sartorial prescriptions and proscriptions designed exactly to avoid dressing in those ways. There's considerable evidence of this approach to dress within the long tradition. The rules of modesty governing (especially) female dress belong here. But that approach is almost always a mistake because it is almost always entwined with the thought, rebutted here, that there are dress norms that are in themselves offerings to idols. But there aren't: *omnia mihi licent.* Any such rules are local, short-lived, and better observed by elegant subversion of local norms than by setting up and enforcing norms of Christian dress that distinguish Christian from pagan flesh at first blush. The liberation of Christian flesh from bondage to sartorial norms goes deep. Christian flesh has been proleptically transfigured, and this means that concern about dress has been removed altogether from the order of being and located entirely in the order of social convention and practical need. One implication of this is that local sartorial norms can be played with rather than worried about. Another, a close cousin of the first, is that Christian flesh acts in accord with its Jesus-cleaved nature when it attends playfully to the gorgeous possibilities of dress without moving imaginations idol-wards. Christian flesh has acquired possibilities of sartorial ornamentation that make even Solomon, in all his sartorial glory, seem unimaginative and underdressed.

5 FOOD

FLESH REQUIRES FOOD AND DRINK, and the taking of these things into the flesh is among the most intimate human fleshly concerns. It's a matter of the lips, the tongue, the throat, and the gut. It involves ingestion, by taking flesh and inanimate matter into one's own flesh; and excretion, by ejecting waste into the world through the urethra and the anus and the mouth. Are there ways of doing these things that glorify Christian flesh, and its LORD to whom it cleaves? And are there fornicatory ways of doing them, ways that idolize or give scandal or both? Is there a Christian grammar of thought about food, and a Christian habitus with respect to it? Are there ways of eating and drinking to which Christian flesh, because it is Christian, turns when it attends to its LORD? And, correspondingly, ways of eating and drinking from which it turns away? Since the eucharist is the fundamental and paradigmatic act of eating for Christians, the first necessary clarification is of its relation to the economy of food and the killing that eating inevitably involves (5.1, 5.2). The second clarification is of the relation of fasting (5.3), required for all Christians, to eucharist and to eating more generally, with a treatment of Dante's Ugolino (5.4) as illustrative of how this relation can be construed and misconstrued. Idolatrous eating, in the form of gluttony (5.5), is sketched by way of its contrast to eucharistic eating; and those forms of eating that might produce scandal (5.6) are depicted in brief.

5.1 Slaughter and Eucharist

We eat and drink: we take solids and liquids into our flesh, usually by way of the mouth. We do it for pleasure, for survival, deliberately, by accident, under compulsion, alone, in company, with and without culinary preparation. We do it regularly and often: eating gives rhythm and order to life. And we do it according to local dietary and commensal norms, which control and restrict what may be eaten, when, and with whom. Codes governing these things are fundamental to the structuring of social life.

Most of what we eat and drink once lived: it had blood and the breath of life, and itself ate other living things; or it had sap and juice, and ate light. These living things are killed in order to be prepared for eating, or are killed in the course of being eaten and digested.

Sometimes, we eat and drink what never lived, and therefore cannot be killed. But this is rare. Most human eating belongs to the economy of death and slaughter: even salt from the sea, synthetics from the laboratory, and water from the underground spring are implicated more or less distantly with death and killing.

Most rarely, we eat what lives without killing it. We ingest parasites without killing them; sometimes they then kill or damage us, and sometimes they then live in symbiotic harmony with us. The LORD gave manna to the Israelites starving in the desert, and in doing so killed nothing. Christian flesh, Jesus-cleaved by baptism, eucharistically eats and drinks Jesus without killing, consuming flesh and blood that cannot die and that brings only life, informing and transfiguring our flesh. These kinds of eating are the only ones fully exempt from the economy of death and slaughter.

Christian flesh has decisively moved from death to life. The deaths it still inflicts and the death it will itself undergo are remnants, threads in a slaughter-fabric being unpicked by Jesus and rewoven into a garment of light and life. We must still eat, which means that we must still participate in the slaughter economy that eating is; and we must still die, which means that we must still contribute our own flesh to that economy when it becomes a corpse. These are necessities, but lamentable ones from which we hope finally to be saved: we pray, as Augustine liked to recommend that we should, in the words of the twenty-fifth Psalm, that we might be delivered from them: *de necessitatibus meis erue me*—deliver me from my necessities.

This prayer has already been answered in the case of eating. Christian flesh already eats Jesus, which is a kind of eating exempt from the economy of death. In the sixth chapter of John's Gospel, this is made explicit: *hic est panis, qui de caelo descendit, non sicut manducaverunt patres et mortui sunt; qui manducat hunc panem, vivet in aeternum*—This is the bread that came down from heaven; it's not like what your ancestors ate, and died; those who eat this bread will live forever. Manna in the desert was a food-gift from the LORD exempt from the economy of death: nothing had to die in order that the Jews could be nourished by it, but that gift did not exempt those who ate it from death. Jesus did have to die in order that his flesh could be eaten: the crucifixion is among the preconditions for the eucharist; but his death was transfigured into life by the resurrection, and then made available after the ascension to Christian flesh, non-bloodily, like manna, altogether outside the economy of death. Jesus's ascended flesh differs from manna in being capable of providing eternal life for those who eat it.

—But isn't bread and wine involved in the eucharist? Doesn't the preparation of those things involve death? Grapes are plucked and crushed; wheat harvested and ground and baked. Isn't the eucharist, too, in these ways implicated in the economy of death?

—It's true that the bread and wine are thus implicated. But they're not what's eaten in the eucharist. What's eaten is the flesh of the ascended Jesus, and what's drunk is his blood. The wheat and grapes have been non-bloodily transfigured and transubstantiated into these, and so the act of eucharistic eating doesn't involve death, even though there is death in its causal backstory, as there is in the backstory of every state of affairs, *post lapsum*. Taking the few steps from pew to altar in order to receive the eucharist involves killing: various small living beings are breathed in and trodden to death. But that is part of the eucharistic backstory in a devastated world; it doesn't belong properly to consuming the eucharist any more than does the crushing of the grapes or the grinding of the wheat.

Lament is the keynote of Christian flesh's participation in the eating that involves slaughter; fasting its ground bass; and the eucharist its grace note.

5.2 Lament

Save the eucharist, there is no properly Christian diet. All foods have been made clean: Christian flesh may keep kosher or observe halal; it may eat vegetarian or paleo or organic; it may renounce gluten or caffeine or alcohol; it may subsist on beef or horsemeat or peanut butter; but it need do none of these things. Jesus-cleaved flesh is bound by no gastronomic obligations in just the same way that it is bound by no sartorial ones (4.6). The LORD expects nothing of us about these things: Christians observe local dietary and commensal norms, abjuring distinctiveness in these matters except where not doing so leads imagination and action idol-wards.

There is distinctiveness, however, in Christian understanding of what it is to eat and drink. If those acts are participant in the economy of death, and if that economy is lamentable because death is lamentable, then Christian eating ought to reflect its participation in that state of affairs. We ordinarily give thanks before we eat: thanks that there is food and drink for us; thanks for the labor participant in preparing it, whether our own or that of others; thanks for the order of the plant and animal worlds that provides food for us; thanks for the gustatory delight we find in eating and for the visual and olfactory delight we take in looking at and smelling food. All this is reasonable and appropriate to Christian flesh: the world is beautiful and bountiful, damaged as it is, and it provides pleasure while sustaining fleshly life.

But Christians ought also to lament the necessity of eating, and of the death handed out by doing it. Table graces should include such laments as complements to gratitude and celebration. As well as thanking the world for our food, Christians ought to lament the killing involved in its eating. Not to do so is to run the risk of naturalizing the slaughter economy involved in eating, of occluding the wound of eating-by-killing that belongs to human flesh, and of encouraging forgetfulness of the paradigmatic primacy of eucharistic eating for Christian flesh.

The fleshly wound of killing by eating goes deep. Our principal mode of relating to flesh other than our own is by slaughter: we've industrialized the killing of plants and animals for our consumption with insouciance and self-congratulation or, more often, without a second thought. But this means that our own flesh, sustained and formed as it is by this killing, is subject to constant and repeated wounding by its unavoidable implication in the killing of what it consumes. A chicken in every pot, a loaf on every table, red meat as often as we can afford it, freshly farmed salmon on the grill—these, for a human population in the billions, mean slaughter on a massive scale performed with precision tools and exactingly systematic methods. We cannot avoid this. We can moderate its savagery by smoothing the way to the abattoir and the threshing floor, but we can't fix it. It's a feature of a fallen and damaged world. Seeing it clearly requires, and sometimes produces, lament. Christian sensibilities about food, formed as they are by eucharistic eating (unbloody, non-slaughterous), should be closely conformed to this view of things. The economy of death that eating is awaits healing; the damage we've done and are doing to living creatures other than ourselves awaits healing; the damage plants and animals do to one another awaits healing; but these healings are beyond our capacity. Our contribution to them now is to attend to them, to notice that they're needed, and to signal our attention by lament. We may also attempt to moderate the suffering involved in killing for food; but we shouldn't, in making these attempts, confuse ourselves into thinking that we can remove what we lament.

5.3   Fasting

We all eat. Some of us also fast. Those who do this deliberately abstain from eating and drinking for a time, whether completely or in part. For all of us, fasting or not, there are periods when we're not eating and drinking; the occurrence of such intervals doesn't by itself constitute a fast. Those who don't eat simply because they have no food also aren't fasting. Fasting happens when local norms and rhythms of eating are deliberately interrupted. "Abstinence from eating meat or another food according to the prescriptions of the conference of bishops is to be observed on Fridays throughout the year," the Catholic Code of Canon Law says: that's a minor fast. Muslims abstain from all food and drink from sunup to sundown during Ramadan: that's a more stringent one. A hunger striker might abstain from all food and drink in order to make a political point: that's a radical fast. Boxers preparing for weigh-in might abstain completely for twenty-four hours; so might those preparing for surgery; and those concerned to lose weight for aesthetic or medical reasons might adopt a diet significantly at odds with local norms and rhythms of eating. Those are all fasts, of varying intensity and duration, and for disparate purposes.

Eating proper to Christian flesh, cleaved to Jesus as it is, is framed and punctuated by fasting. Jesus fasted in his natal flesh, most dramatically during the temptations in the desert. Eucharistic eating is prepared for by fasting for at least one hour, as the Catholic Code requires, and this is one indicator of the difference between what's eaten in the eucharist and what's eaten otherwise. An important part of the difference is exactly that what's eaten otherwise unavoidably involves death, whereas what's eaten eucharistically involves only life; fasting marks this difference by requiring those who eat Jesus, the bread of heaven, to separate their ordinary eatings from their eucharistic eatings, and to chastise the former by the latter. The seasons of penance during the liturgical year (Fridays, Lent, Advent) are also marked by fasting, and for similar reasons: preparing for life includes and requires abstention from the economy of death. The local rhythms and norms of eating, for Christians, are, therefore, interwoven with and shown for what they are by the universal rhythms and norms of the fast.

Fasting disciplines culinary and gastronomic passions. This is the purpose for which it's most often recommended in manuals of ascetical theology and in the compendia of sayings of the desert fathers, many of whom were virtuosos of the fast. Syncletica, the abbess of a monastery/hermitage in Egypt in (perhaps) the fourth century, is said to have said: "The pleasures and riches of the world must not attract you as if they were of any use to you. Because of its pleasure the art of cooking is respected, but by rigorous fasting you should trample on that pleasure. Never have enough bread to satisfy you and do not long for wine." This is representative, and there is something to be said for it. Intense and repeated fasting may discipline the passions in these ways, and gluttons may need such discipline. But fasting also increases gastronomic pleasure: eating after a fast provides an intensity of delight in what's eaten that those who have never fasted and always had more than enough to eat are unable to match or perhaps to imagine. Fasting can be an exercise for the gastronomic voluptuary as much as for the ascetical virtuoso. Pleasure in eating and drinking, too, is neither inevitably a distraction from the LORD nor a movement of the imagination idol-wards. The ascetical, stoical justification for fasting is of limited value, and itself easily becomes a distortedly voluptuous idolatry of food.

A fuller and more precise depiction of fasting's purposes requires both eschatology and sacramental theology.

Eschatology: Christian flesh, Jesus-cleaved, is going somewhere: first to death, a return to body-as-corpse; and then to life eternal, as resurrected flesh clothed with light and sensorily and intellectually intimate with the ascended flesh of Jesus in a manner that fulfills both its baptismal cleaving to that flesh and its earthly eucharistic eating of it. Fasting, in counterpoint to slaughterous eating here below, permits Christian flesh to participate temporarily in the economy of life to which it is called and toward which it moves. There is no heavenly eating as we understand eating: no killing for consumption and no need to sustain the resurrected fleshly body with food. Plants eat light now, by photosynthesis; in something like that way, we shall then eat the LORD's light, by graceful permission and with grateful consumption; that will meet our resurrected flesh's desires and exceed its needs. Fasting throws the slaughter economy of eating into relief by permitting those who fast to enter, temporarily, into a different economy; this is an epistemic benefit. It also permits those who fast to enter, for a while, into that state of being in which death-food is neither given nor taken, by strict analogy with the heavenly end of marriage, as Matthew writes in the twenty-second chapter of his Gospel: "in the resurrection they neither marry nor are given in marriage, but are like the angels in heaven." The angels in heaven not only don't marry; they also don't eat plants or animals because they subsist on the LORD's light. So also for us, and fasting shows us this. The discipline fasting brings to the gluttonous passions is a benefit ancillary to the more fundamental gifts given by the act of fasting.

Sacramental theology: Fasting is temporary abstention, abstention preceded by eating and with renewed eating in view. Were it to be abstention without an end in view, it would be suicide rather than fasting. When, as is usual in the devastation, the eating that follows fasting is death-involved in the double sense given (it requires the death of others and is done to stave off our own), breaking the fast means abandoning one economy—that of life—for another—that of death. But when fasting is ended by eating Jesus's flesh, the economy of life is not left behind. In the devastation, fasting finds its proper end in the eucharist. That is not because the passions have been disciplined by the fast (though that may have happened). It is because those who fast have been prepared by their fast for real gastronomic intimacy with the ascended LORD: they have been, in a small way, purged, which is to say purified. The rhythm of fasting and eucharistic eating in the devastation participates in the inbreathing of light and the outbreathing of praise which is proper to the life of the world to come.

Fasting shows the meaning of, and prepares for, the only life-giving eating we can do in the world of death and slaughter. That's why, for Christians, fasting is not a matter for lament. Jesus is said to prescribe this in the sixth chapter of Matthew's Gospel: "When you fast, don't look sad like hypocrites; they disfigure (*demoliuntur*) their faces so that they seem to others to be fasting. . . . Instead, when you fast anoint your head and wash your face so that you won't be seen by others to be fasting, but rather by your Father, who is hidden (*absconditus*)." What's rejected here is public lament for the fast as a grimly penitential work; what's affirmed is offering the fast to the LORD in free and delighted gratitude for the possibility of leaving death-eating behind. This is a hidden gratitude, given to a hidden LORD, because it has no purchase on or place in a devastated world in which what's evident is only death and its concomitants: *mortui enim estis, et vita vestra abscondita est cum Christo in Deo—* you are dead, and your lives are hidden with Christ in God.

It isn't that Christian flesh ought to fast. Fasting is no duty for it. Rather, it's that Jesus-cleaved flesh fasts out of gratitude for the gift of food free from death and slaughter. Fasting is, for Christian flesh, like the white baptismal garment, which is donned because it is fitting. Jerome shows how these things fit together in a letter to Fabiola: "When we're ready to put on Christ (*cum parati ad indumentum Christi*) we will have put off the tunics of skin (*tunicas pelliceas deposuerimus*) and will then have a linen garment put on us (*induemur veste linea*) which is in itself death-free (*nihil in se mortis habens*) and wholly white (*tota candida*)." Jerome, along with most of his contemporaries, both Christian and pagan, thought of linen as intrinsically death-free because no animals died to make it. He did not consider plant death to be death, and he's wrong about that, but the force of his point survives the error: a baptismal garment free from the economy of death fits the flesh of the baptizand because baptism takes the baptizand out of the economy of death and into that of life. Putting on the white garment, or having it put on, suits Christian flesh. It's not required, and therefore not a matter of precept: rather, it suits the flesh it clothes. *Tunicae pelliceae* don't suit; when they're worn by Christians, as sometimes they are, they speak against Christian flesh, and are, when they can't be avoided and are seen clearly for what they are, an occasion for lament. The same structure of thought is evident in and properly applicable to Christian eating: the rhythm of fasting/eucharist suits: that rhythm, like (Jerome's understanding of) what's needed to make linen, is outside the cycle of slaughter; other eatings don't suit, even though they're unavoidable. They're necessities we pray and hope to be delivered from. Leather shoes, veal chops, and arugula-laced quinoa are all, in this respect, in the same category.

Fasting, as a grace note to the eating done by Christian flesh, has eucharistic eating as its purposeful end.

5.4 Ugolino and the Eucharist

Toward the end of Dante's *Inferno*, in the thirty-second canto, Dante (the poem's pilgrim, not its author) encounters Ugolino, who is repeatedly eating flesh torn with his teeth from another man's brain stem. Ugolino is energetic in this work; he eats flesh "as bread is eaten (*manduca*) in hunger"—the verb is the same as that used in the sixth chapter of John's Gospel for eucharistic eating. His damnation is endlessly to repeat this cannibalistic cycle, and to perform in doing so a bloodily repetitive reversal of the unbloody eucharistic eating recommended by John's Jesus. Put to the question by Dante the pilgrim, Ugolino explains, self-justifyingly, why his damnation takes this form. The man whose flesh he's eating—one Ruggieri—had, in life, imprisoned Ugolino and four of his offspring in a tower, and there left them to starve. The children die, serially, on the fourth, fifth, and sixth days after the door is locked; Ugolino lasts a little longer, and dies on the eighth day. As hunger begins to bite, the children weep and implore, but Ugolino, according to the account he provides Dante, does not: he has become unyielding, stone-like—he has only a stony heart to offer to his children in exchange for their request for bread (a clear echo of Jesus asking who among fathers would give their children a stone if they asked for bread). Neither does he speak to his dying offspring, though they beg him to. Instead, he gnaws on his own hands, and the children, interpreting this as a sign of his hunger, offer their own flesh to him as remedy: "Father," they say, "we'd suffer less if you'd eat us. You clothed us in this miserable flesh—now strip it off." Ugolino doesn't, and also doesn't respond to them in any other way, whether with speech, tears, or caresses. Only when they're all dead can he speak to them. Ugolino concludes his story by saying, ambiguously, about the period between the death of the last child and his own, "Then fasting overpowered grief"—or, possibly, "Then fasting did what grief could not." The line can be read to suggest that his fast killed him when his grief could not; or that his fast ended in eating the now-dead bodies of his offspring, an offer he'd been unable to accept—because of grief?—when they were still living. On the second reading, he eats their dead bodies after refusing their living flesh, an act of eating that precedes his own death and his cannibalistic damnation.

This story is preceded by the pilgrim's oath that he will, if Ugolino can convince him that there's just cause for his hatred of Ruggieri, make the story known to the world. And he does that, *in extenso*, in the thirty-third canto of the *Inferno*. Dante (the poet) shows, by providing the story, Dante (the pilgrim) as having been convinced, by the heartrending story, of the justice of Ugolino's flesh-gnawing hatred of Ruggieri. Nevertheless, Ugolino is damned, along with the other traitors in their many kinds, frozen (hell's floor is icy in the *Inferno*) into an endless cycle of cannibalistic revenge upon his killer, and so Dante (the poet's) readers are at once offered indignation at what Ruggieri did to Ugolino and his children, sympathy for the sufferings they underwent, and an uneasy sense that Dante (the pilgrim) must have made some mistake in being convinced by Ugolino's self-justifying story if the bloody particulars of Ugolino's damnation are to make sense. He's not just damned for being a traitor; the flesh-eating aspect of his damnation means that something, in life, went wrong with his eating. But what?

The story Ugolino tells can be read as a eucharistic one, even though neither he nor his hearer is shown as so understanding it, and the reader is left in doubt as to whether this is how to read it. The reading I'm about to give won't, and shouldn't, remove that doubt. The reading is intended, rather, to heighten the tension provided by the story to those who read or hear it, and thereby to show the contours of the story's difficulty.

Stripped to the bone, the story is about fasting that could have ended in eating living and life-giving flesh, but that ended instead in eating dead bodies that bring death. Ugolino is offered life-giving flesh by his children, and he cannot accept it; his inability to accept it is correlated with his inability to mourn as those who offer themselves to him do—they weep; he doesn't—and with his inability to speak their names—they call upon him; he remains silent. Ugolino's stony silence is matched by his inability to receive the gift offered. He weeps only after his children are dead, and then he can eat them. But what he eats then is dead, and it yields for him only death and an unquenchable revengeful desire for living flesh, the simulacrum of which (Ruggieri's brain stem) he gets and eats forever in hell.

So read, the story dramatizes the archetypal structure of Christian eating, which is the fast leading to the eucharist. Fasting prepares for eucharist; eucharist is living flesh willingly offered, flesh exempt from the cycle of slaughter; accepting the offer requires repentance (*non sum dignus* . . .), tears, and the calling of the name of the one—Jesus—offering it; the offer, when accepted by eating, takes the eater out of the cycle of slaughter. Ugolino refuses the offer and is thereby sunk deep into that repetitive cycle, as the particulars of his damnation show.

But the story is unbearable. How could it have been a good thing for Ugolino to eat the flesh of his still-living children? Dante's (the poet's) story shows us a devastated world in which the Guelphs and the Ghibellines, the likes of Ugolino and Ruggieri, constantly murder, betray, rape, torture, and starve one another. One response to that world is to enter fully into its violence by contributing to it, stonily, without lament: revenge is at the heart of that response. You tear the flesh that tears yours, and you refuse to weep while doing it, glorying in the justice of your act and glorying, too, in your capacity to do it. Another is to receive remorsefully, and with full acknowledgment of the wounds involved, deep, bloody, and fatal as they are, living flesh whose implication in the economy of slaughter has been transfigured by the unbloody willingness with which it gives itself to that slaughter: eucharist is at the heart of that response. You acknowledge that flesh-tearing is useless and never ending; you acknowledge your own incapacity to do anything else; and you weep, tears without end. Both responses are wounding, agonizing. But the first perpetuates slaughter, while the second ends it. For Ugolino to weep, to call his children by name, and to eat their living flesh freely offered, would have been to enter into a eucharistic economy, an economy participant in that constituted by the natal flesh of Jesus, freely offered. He couldn't. And so he was damned. His damnation was his incapacity to receive living flesh, which is to say his incapacity to receive Jesus.

5.5   Gluttony

Even though all foods are clean for Christians, it's still possible for Christians to eat meretriciously. One clear way of doing this is to eat and drink as though those acts were self-sufficient, without purpose, point, or meaning beyond the doing of them. Those who eat in this way need no table grace, whether of lament or thanks; they don't frame or interpret their eating by preparing for it as if it was for anything other than itself; they simply eat, sometimes to excess and sometimes insufficiently, but always inordinately because ordered eating is, for Christians, articulated with and participatory in the rhythm of fasting and eucharist, while meretricious eating, to the extent that it is meretricious, is separated from that economy.

A good word for this kind of meretricious eating is gluttony, which is derived distantly from the Latin *gula*, which means, among pagans, "throat" or "oesophagus," and thereby the site of appetite for food. This pagan Latin word became, among Christians, the standard term for a disordered habit of eating and drinking, and then informed, accruing connotations as it did so, the English "gluttony" and "glutton."

Gluttons may kill or damage themselves by eating too much or eating too little, but not all who do those things are gluttons, and gluttons need do neither.

Gluttons are, rather, those whose appetites for food and drink are recursive: they eat and drink only to eat and drink; the meaning of their eating and drinking is given solely by the acts themselves, remembered from the past and anticipated in the future. Gluttons are like those who speak only to hear their own voices or those who caress only for the haptic sensations it provides their own flesh. Habitual gluttony, habitual recursive eating, is a vice; when Christians do it, it is meretricious: it speaks directly against the Christ-clothed and Christ-cleaved identity of the flesh that eats. It stands in fornicatorily direct opposition to the rhythm of fasting and eucharist that is the paradigm of Christian eating, and does so in idolatrous form. Eating is, for gluttons, a thoroughgoing idol.

—But surely the usual sense of "gluttony" (and *gula*) isn't exactly that, but rather immoderate eating, eating to excess? That's how it's depicted in Christian art, for example in the panel devoted to *gula* in Hieronymus Bosch's "Table of the Seven Deadly Sins," where the obesity and drunkenness produced by excess are the point. Thomas Aquinas, too, in *Summa Theologiae* 2/2.148, which is devoted to the topic, understands *gula* largely in this way, as a disordered desire (*concupiscentia*) for food, which leads, ordinarily, to an immoderate delight (*immoderata delectatio*) in the act of eating, in the tactile and gustatory pleasures of taking food into the mouth and then chewing and swallowing it, and thus to eating too much. Wouldn't it therefore be better, more in accord with the long tradition and with ordinary English usage, to reserve "gluttony" (and *gula*) for eating to excess?

—That's certainly possible. It's true that this is the sense of the words dominant among Christians, and, largely, in ordinary English usage. But there are advantages to using "gluttony" to think about and label what is for Christians a more fundamentally meretricious approach to eating and drinking. One is that it helps Christians to see that eating more than is needed for sustaining the body isn't by itself meretricious; if that were the case, then seeking and finding delight in food and drink and in company to share them would always be so, and that is not a conclusion supportable by Christian thought even though it has often been attractive to Christians. The pleasure given by food and drink is a good proper to fleshly creatures, and should be celebrated as such, even when it is also, and properly, lamented for its inextricable entwining with slaughter. Overindulgence, whether in quantity of food or in attention to its particular qualities, becomes fornicatory rather than glorious when it flows from eating recursively, idolatrously, as though eating justified and explained itself. Another advantage is that using "gluttony" in this way indicates a commonplace, which is that disordered desire for food can as easily show itself in eating less than is needed as in eating more. The bulimic and the anorectic rival or outdo the gourmand in their attention to eating's particulars as though those particulars were all that mattered. They're all gluttons, and calling them so is illuminating of and attentive to a grammar of Christian thought about food and eating deeper than the one implied by limiting gluttony to overindulgence.

When an action is undertaken as if it had no end or point or purpose external to itself, finding a reason to stop doing it is difficult. A body in motion needs something external to itself to stop it moving: a tennis ball hit on a rising trajectory across the net would, in a world without atmosphere or gravity or any solid object to get in the way, continue moving for ever, *sine fine*. The glutton eating, likewise: were the cook Strega Nona, were the belly infinitely expandable, were the spaghetti bowl infinitely large, were there no need to defecate or vomit, and were the restaurant never to close, the glutton of excess would eat forever. There'd be no reason to stop. The glutton of privation would likewise endlessly eat and regurgitate, or sit at table resolutely not eating, world without end. Recursive appetites like gluttony tend toward insatiability just because they are recursive. Their indulgence is brought to an end, when it is, by something that from the glutton's point of view is an interference from without. This is the heart of gluttony's idolatrous fornication: it's not that gluttons find excessive pain or pleasure in eating and drinking, though they may; it's not that they eat too much or too little, though they may; it's that, for them, eating and drinking are removed from any economy—that of slaughter as much as that of gift—external to those acts, and are thereby made into freestanding idols. Like all idols, food and drink, when so understood, demand final and complete loyalty. Gluttons want to ingest and regurgitate the cosmos.

Insatiability is intimate with solitude. Gluttons, of whatever stripe, always eat alone even when others are present. Why would they need company? What matters is ingestion, maximized or minimized; what's attended to is food, by itself; other people, if attended to as fellow eaters, distract. Gluttons don't seek solitude because of shame at their unusual eating habits, though that may be present in gluttony's early stages. Once the habit has gone deep, it makes both shame and company irrelevant. Gluttons can be at banquet tables with a hundred others, and still nothing is present to them but the food. This is another aspect of gluttony's meretriciousness: glorious eating, in contrast, has the presence of others as proper to it. The eucharist is never consumed alone, and for those whose eating is formed according to the Christian rhythm of fasting and eucharist, the presence of others at the table belongs properly to eating. The bread broken and shared, whether eucharistically or at a non-eucharistic table with friends, isn't merely chewed, swallowed, and digested; it's exactly shared, extended into an economy of making and use and cooperation outside itself. That's essential to the eating that conforms to Christian flesh, and the contrast with gluttony's meretriciousness goes deep.

There are literary gluttons of excess (Rabelais's Gargantua most obviously; Shakespeare's Falstaff, perhaps; Fielding's Tom Jones, sometimes), but surprisingly few—far fewer than there are literary representations of the avaricious or the lustful. There's no one among literary gluttons to rival the baroque fleshly inventiveness of De Sade's protagonists, nor even the lesser imaginativeness of the many literary and filmic Casanovas and Don Juans, nor the miserliness of Balzac's *Père Goriot*. But there are some suggestive minor portraits. One is Mrs. Clennam in Dickens's *Little Dorrit*. She's a woman in her sixties, perhaps, long widowed; she lives alone, attended by one ancient servant; she hasn't left her room for more than a dozen years; and is "beyond the reach of all changing emotions," frozen into stasis like (Dickens doesn't say) Satan in the ice of Dante's *Inferno*. Her habits of eating show what she is. They are a matter of immovable routine and deep solitude. At eleven in the morning she is served, alone, oysters, "eight in number, circularly set out on a white plate on a tray covered with a white napkin, flanked by a slice of buttered French roll, and a little compact glass of cool wine and water." At nine in the evening she is served, again alone, "a dish of little rusks and a small precise pat of butter, cool, symmetrical, white, and plump," together with a "hot and odorous mixture" of port, lemon, sugar, and spices, "measured out and compounded with as much nicety as a physician's prescription." Every detail matters: the temperature of the liquids, the shape and texture of the solids, the arrangement of the receptacles and utensils on the tray used to bring her food. Most telling: Mrs. Clennam sometimes doesn't eat what she's brought, and when she doesn't, she "places the act to her credit in her Eternal Day-Book." She is not a glutton of the large, excessive gesture, like Gargantua; neither is she a glutton of self-erasure, like Kafka's hunger artist. She's a glutton of precision: the food is what matters, in all its particulars. It can be eaten, or not; but it must be brought and placed, received in solitude, and contemplated recursively as matter self-enclosed. The picture chills because of the smallness of its scale, and the precision with which it's used to show how food can contribute to, and show, a soul's damnation.

5.6 Scandalous Eating

Gluttony isn't the only mode of meretricious eating that speaks against Christian flesh. There are also eatings and drinkings that cause scandal, as Paul puts it in the Corinthian correspondence (3.2). These incline the imagination, whether of those who eat or those who see them doing so, toward idols. Gluttonous eating is idolatrous in itself; but it may not seem so to those who observe it (would Mrs. Clennam's eatings so seem?), and, strictly, it doesn't turn the imaginations of the gluttonous anywhere. They're already sufficiently sunk in idolatry that they can see nothing but the food they're eating; their imagination needs no kindling. Scandalous eatings and drinkings, in contrast, are those that cause others to turn away from the LORD and toward idols. Eatings of this kind are unfitting for Christian flesh; teeth that chew Christ and throats that swallow him don't easily, fittingly, coherently, chew and swallow in these ways.

One idol is wanton slaughter, the taking of life as if it were pleasurable or a matter of no account. Slaughter is inseparable from most eating (5.1), so eating that befits Christian flesh doesn't seek to avoid it. Avoidance is impossible. What Christian flesh does when it is fully responsive to the gift of food is lament the slaughter it cannot avoid. That is the essential thing. But there are features of a transnational system of food production and food delivery that make lament difficult. Notably, those systems obscure the fact that slaughter on a massive scale is involved in getting food to those who'll eat it. Packaging and presentation, whether at the supermarket, the restaurant, or in the box delivered to your door, emphasize, in varying degrees and proportions, gastronomic delight, the benefit of health, and the good life led by the creatures who died for this product (smiling pigs, amber waves of grain, cage-free chickens who know their mothers' names). A good deal of trouble is taken not to show the abattoir, the chickens stacked immovably on top of one another in the warehouse, the salmon farmed at close quarters and killed without being able to breed, and all the other horrors of industrialized slaughter. Insouciant complicity with these systems of food production and distribution erases lament, and thereby speaks against Christian flesh. That is a truth in the order of being. But because, as is usual, there's no direct transition from the order of being to the order of knowing, nothing much immediately follows about the scandalousness of unthinking complicity in slaughter-blind economies of food production.

In order for a Christian's purchase and consumption of, for example, factory-farmed meat to give scandal in the Pauline sense—to move the imaginations of those who see it done toward idols, to understand the meat eaten to have been sacrificed to idols—a good deal of knowledge must be in place. When it is not, when most people locally, Christian and pagan, do not see or understand the economy in which they participate, they won't be scandalized by seeing that Christians, too, participate in that economy without apparent second thought. No scandal is given in such a situation. Similarly, when Christians are themselves without sufficient food to maintain health, and in more extreme cases without sufficient food to maintain life (perhaps one-quarter of Christians worldwide are in one or another of these cases), they won't be scandalized by seeing the participation of Christians in a slaughter-blind economy. They're more likely to be scandalized by seeing other Christians gourmandize while they suffer or starve. And that is an altogether different set of scandals.

Abiding by local norms of food production that occlude slaughter at their heart, and that, in part for the same reasons, guarantee an excess of food for some and inadequate nourishment for others, isn't adiaphorous for Christian flesh. The patterns of reasoning that inform and suggest such norms aren't possible patterns of reasoning for Christians, and when, and to the extent that, their Christian flesh has become comfortable for them, Christians don't use or assent to them. They find themselves instead drawn, like moths to a flame, to open acknowledgment of and lament for the slaughter and suffering proper to the economy of eating, and to resistance to the occlusions of those states of affairs. How this looks in particular cases depends on local variables.

There's also the question of scandalous local commensal norms. These may be taken by those who observe them to be incised into the world's order and sanctioned by violence. Christians may then judge that the decision to abide by them, or not, isn't adiaphorous. To abide by them might be to support a local commensal norm that speaks against being Jesus-cleaved because it moves the imagination idol-wards—the idol in this case being the thought that there are commensal norms that bind everyone, including Christians, which is to say exceptionless commensal norms. Better than this, more coherent with being Jesus-cleaved, would be to adopt commensal styles that signal the conventionality and transgressibility of all commensal norms. Doing so in such a context is consistent with the commensal practice of Jesus in his natal flesh. He was, Scripture repeatedly shows, consistent and dramatic in transgressing local commensal norms, and those whose flesh is cleaved to his are likely to be so too, especially when such norms are exclusionary.

—But surely this view can be taken as a precept, a requirement, something asked of the Jesus-cleaved? Perhaps it could be formulated like this: you should transgress commensal norms when they represent themselves as natural, part of the order of things. But if this is the point, then Christians are as much subject to commensal custom as anyone else; their commensal behavior is ordered by precept as much as anyone else's; and their commensal behavior is as particular as anyone else's.

—No, it isn't necessary to see the matter in this way. A first example. There are exclusionary local régimes governing commensality that present themselves as belonging to the order of things. Men and women, for instance, may be locally forbidden to eat with one another; so may people with different skin colors, different languages, different patterns of understanding and relating to the LORD. Brahmins do not eat with non-Brahmins; Orthodox Jews find themselves defiled by eating the wrong foods off the wrong plates with the wrong people at the wrong time. People may choose not to eat with, or feel themselves defiled by eating with, people whose dietary habits are different. There are vegetarians and vegans who won't eat with meat eaters, or at a table at which meat is served. These are all norms about commensality, and when they're backed with the imagination that they're rooted in differences in the natures of those with whom table-sharing appears impossible, or are understood to be matters of divine command, of rational necessity, or of the order of civilization, then offences against them are likely to lead to violence or other extreme sanctions. These are not possible patterns of reasoning for Christians; Jesus has overturned them, and Christian flesh, even when it abides by such norms locally, as it may, is not bound by them. Abiding by such commensal norms, even when done by Christians, is always ideal-typically, even if not always actually, a matter of observing local conventions with local utility. Such observance is ordinarily adiaphorous for Christians; being cleaved to Jesus has liberated us from taking such norms with deep seriousness. Christians, when their Jesus-cleaved flesh becomes comfortable to them, eat happily with anyone at all.

—Doesn't this understanding of how Christian flesh responds to norms of commensality have implications for eucharistic eating? If the single most characteristic commensal habit of Christians is openness, a manifestation of which is their abiding by local restrictive commensal norms as non-binding conventions, might this not mean that the restriction of eucharistic eating to Christian flesh ought to be abandoned, and the invitation to the eucharistic feast made universal?

—That seems right. But it doesn't entail, nor even suggest, that the unbaptized ought to be encouraged to consume the consecrated elements at the eucharist. Christian flesh eats what it is: cleaved to Jesus, its limbs having become limbs of his flesh, it eats exactly that flesh, the flesh it is a limb of. The unbaptized, when they consume the consecrated host at a eucharist, or drink the consecrated wine, do not do what Christians do. They perform a different act. They don't eat Jesus's flesh, because a condition necessary for doing that is being cleaved to Jesus by baptism. Those not so cleaved eat and drink, instead, bread and wine. The commensal regulations that hedge the eucharist—it's only for the baptized; others may ask a blessing but should not consume—recognize and display this state of affairs. The regulations don't place a ban so much as acknowledge and describe and communicate an impossibility. This way of thinking about the restriction of the eucharist to the baptized preserves its openness to all because the necessary condition for receiving it (baptism) is itself without restriction: any human can receive that, and with ease. It also has the implication (an important one) that when the commensal discipline of the eucharist is breached, as it often is, Christians can rest easy. There is no need for violent policing of commensal boundaries, and no need for lament if those boundaries are breached. The worst that can happen is that some eat bread and drink wine, while others eat and drink Jesus. The churches ought nevertheless to maintain in teaching and practice the restriction (which is really the openness) of eucharistic eating to the baptized. Doing so configures the form of the rite to its reality, and permits continued awareness on everyone's part of the radical importance of baptism as the means by which Christian flesh is made.

There are, with respect to Christian eating as with respect to every other mode of Christian fleshly action, no precepts, rules, or duties. Instead there are sketches, pictorial or verbal, of what the holiness of Christian flesh looks like—of how Christian flesh, when it is attentive to the Jesus to whom it is cleaved, eats. Those sketches are hagiographies; they show something altogether outside the sphere of the command, even when what they show can be reduced to a code of conduct (always with loss, and usually with something worse, the occlusion of the gift relation that makes creatures what they are). In this case, the case of eating, a brief hagiography looks like this: Christian flesh acts in accord with what it is when it abides by the rhythm of fast and eucharist; when it laments the slaughter inseparable from its eating and is unhinged by the wound of that slaughter's extent and unavoidability; when it delights in the pleasures of eating; when it resists modes of production and distribution of food that occlude the economy of slaughter, or that increase it beyond need; when it resists radicalized commensal restrictions by embracing commensal openness; when it resists economies that guarantee hunger or starvation for some and excess for others; and when, in every act of eating, it refuses idolatry of food and instead gives glory to the LORD.

6 CARESSES

HUMAN FLESH is essentially and constitutively ecstatically erotic; it receives itself as flesh by way of the caress, and gives fleshliness to others in the same way (1.4). But caresses are, after the fall, damaged: never pure gifts, but always also wounds (6.1). Tactile connection damages flesh as much and as often as it constitutes and heals it. The capacity of flesh to wound is transfigured, but not erased, when it is cleaved to Jesus; such cleaving opens to it new possibilities of caressing in both gift and receipt, and calls others into question (6.2, 6.3). Being cleaved to Jesus shows, too, with a new clarity, what fornicatory caresses are, in both their purely idolatrous and their scandalous forms, and opens some new ways toward their redress (6.4, 6.5).

6.1 Caresses and Wounds

Flesh, along with everything else, was damaged by the primordial cataclysm of the fall. So Christians think. The principal evidence of this damage, evident to all, is flesh's fragility and mortality (1.5). Flesh is subject to damage from within, by aging and other kinds of internally generated decay, and from without, by the violence of the world. Jesus's natal flesh (2.1) wasn't damaged in these ways; it suffered and died by permission rather than by subjection, and in this shows to Christians that human flesh is not intrinsically or inevitably subject to those things. Fragility and mortality are not, however, the only kinds of damage flesh underwent at the fall. Damage was done also to the fleshly capacity to give and receive caresses. The flesh-constituting gift of the caress can no longer, since the cataclysm, be given or received as simple gift; the loving touch of the caress is now always also the scarifying touch of the wound. All caresses, now, are wound-inflected; and some fleshly touches, now, are effectively (if not intrinsically) nothing but wounds, successful in killing—removing altogether, if temporarily, from fleshly existence—those who receive them. None of this was possible before the fall, nor will be in the resurrection. Then, all caresses, which will be many and intense and delightful, will be pure gifts, non-scarifying, flesh-constituting, flesh-sustaining, and flesh-enhancing; and then there will be no possibility of the touch that kills, because mortality is ruled out. Jesus's natal flesh shows this, too: the caresses he gives do nothing other than heal and bless. Whenever he is touched or touches, those are the results; and there is no record, nor any possibility, of his natal flesh inflicting wounds. The infliction of wounds is not the same as violence: in a fallen, wounded, and wounding world, force may need to be used to heal and bless, and there are indications that Jesus's natal flesh used it, for example in the scouring of the temple precincts. But wounds are nothing other than damage, and those Jesus's natal flesh received but did not give.

"Concupiscence" is a good shorthand label, and one with a long pedigree, for the damage that flesh has undergone with respect to the caress. The word directly indicates an intense, avid desire: "cupidity" has the same Latin root, and it preserves better than does "concupiscence" the sense, in English, of urgent greed, which is also proper to concupiscence. "Concupiscence" also connotes a possessive, expropriative mode of desiring. Flesh, when concupiscent, wants what it wants for itself alone, as a possession solely owned, something to which it alone has title; and it wants it urgently, now, without interference. Examples are easy to come by: infants' desires for the breast and its milk are like this; so are gluttons' for the salty, cool oysterflesh in the mouth, chased by the cold, aromatic wine; so are lovers' for the beloved's flesh under the hand, yielding to the caress; so are schoolyard bullies' for the victim's soft belly pummelled by the fist; so are rapists' for the violation of their prey's flesh; and so are murderers' for the life leaving the flesh of the victim under their hands.

These are relatively pure instances of the concupiscent touch. They share some features, most obviously that of potential or actual violence aimed at the pseudo-pleasure of gratification. If anything obstructs that gratification—prevents the infant from sucking, the rapist from violating, the murderer from killing, the bully from humiliating—the result is the use of force, whenever possible, to remove the obstacle. The examples also share tactility: they are works of the flesh directed toward other flesh, and what they seek is the immediacy of a certain kind of touch. They also share a tendency toward solipsism: concupiscent flesh is concerned principally, and sometimes only, with its own gratification, which is to say not at all with the gifts it may give or the damage it may do to the recipient of its wounding caress. The teeth masticating the body that was once an oyster's flesh don't lament the killing that preceded and made possible the eating; bullies don't lament the pain they're inflicting on the flesh of those they torment because that pain and its concomitant humiliation is what they want; and rapists have no concern for the violent damage they inflict on the flesh of those they rape, except insofar as that damage provides gratification to themselves.

Expropriation, violence, tactility, solipsism: these are the hallmarks of the concupiscent caress, which also, and unavoidably, wounds what it touches. In its ideal type, the concupiscent caress erases what it touches. That is its proper goal. Complete possession entails erasure of the other as other by its absorption without remainder into the fleshly ambit of the concupiscent one. If anything of the other remains outside that ambit, as a genuine other, then it hasn't been fully expropriated, fully taken from the public sphere into that of private ownership. Expropriation-as-erasure can be brought about by ingestion: to eat the flesh of the one you caress, to make that caress exactly a matter of lips and tongue and teeth and throat, is to remove its otherness by incorporating it into yourself. Killing without eating has something of the same effect. Flesh concupiscently caressed to the point of taking its life has also been expropriated in the sense that nothing of it remains in the public sphere: it has become a corpse, beyond the possibility of returning the caress or receiving itself as flesh from the caress. What concupiscent caresses seek, and what they can never finally have, is the erasure of everything within reach (the flesh concerns itself as flesh only with what's within reach) that might initiate or return the caress. Were anything of that kind to remain, with it would remain something alive that is not wholly owned, and that would exactly mean that flesh's concupiscence had found a limit. It always, fortunately, does: no flesh has the capacity to make the world into a simple occasion for its own gratification.

Three fleshly scenes that approach what concupiscence seeks without ever quite arriving there: the slave quarters, in which all the flesh within reach stands ready as an occasion for solipsistic concupiscent gratification, and can be killed should it refuse; the abattoir, in which all the flesh at hand has been slaughtered as preparation for ingestion by concupiscent flesh; and the supermarket-as-cornucopia, in which all the bodies before the eye are set out before the concupiscent gaze and within reach of the purchasing hand. In all these cases, concupiscent flesh finds its harem. Nothing arrayed in these spectacular scenes can return the caress, which is the state of affairs that flesh, under the sign of concupiscence, avidly seeks, but which its concupiscence prevents.

But the harem and the abattoir are not what flesh really seeks, even at its most concupiscent. These spectacles are the proper end of the caress-as-wound, but when they're arrived at, when flesh is transfixed by force into an array whose sole purpose is to provide an object for the solipsistic gratification of the one who staged it, the array turns out to disappoint. That is because flesh cannot, now, once transfixed and staged, provide the caress; in transfixing it, the concupiscent one has turned it into a thing that can receive wounds, but that can return nothing. Necrophilia is the extreme case and the logical culmination of this state of affairs. A corpse can be caressed, in a way; the simulacrum of a caress can be offered to it. But it returns nothing. It cannot provide the caress that even the most disorderedly concupiscent flesh in fact needs (and implicitly wants) in order to live. The concupiscent fleshly caress fails, therefore, in direct proportion to its concupiscence. It is, in almost pure form, a performatively incoherent act.

In the devastated world we find ourselves in, there are no caresses entirely free of concupiscence; none, therefore, that do not also in some measure wound. But there are also no fleshly gestures that are concupiscent without remainder. Concupiscence can certainly achieve its goal of expropriating the flesh before it, which it does most completely by killing. But even when that has been achieved, when the necrophiliacs are caressing their corpses and the slave masters their slaves, the caresses thus offered have in them some trace of glory, no matter how exiguous. That is because of the convertibility of the transcendentals, and, what is the same, the nullity of evil. Goodness and being and beauty are, in the order of being, convertible one with another: to be is to be good, and to be good is to be beautiful; the extent to which any particular is the one is the extent to which it is the other. And, correspondingly, the extent to which it has been damaged—has lost or failed ever to have goods proper to it—is the extent to which it lacks goodness and beauty. Complete loss of being-goodness-beauty entails nonexistence: evil is absence rather than presence, nothing rather than something, *nihil* rather than *res*. But then, even the concupiscent caress that wounds, that intends the erasure of the flesh it touches—even that gesture has some goods in it just because it is not a simple absence. When the necrophiliac reaches out his hand to caress the corpse's cheek, what's offered is at best the simulacrum of a caress because there's no flesh to hand. But what the necrophiliac does is not nothing. It's an intentional action exhibiting sufficient order and, thus, sufficient goodness and beauty, to prosecute its intention. The intention is recursively self-defeating, and to the degree that that's so succeeds in erasing itself. But it doesn't completely succeed in self-erasure, and even to the observer there are evident in it traces, vestiges, remnants of what the ordinary caress of a living face would look like. Those traces are what make the pseudo-caresses offered by a necrophiliac so horrible: they show how close the fleshly intimacies of the torturer with the tortured are to those lavished on the beloved by the lover. The skull shows always through the skin; but the skull also shows the shape of the face it makes. The fall's devastation does not erase the beauty and goodness of creation; and the wounds offered by flesh to flesh do not erase the beauty of the caress. Were erasure to happen in either case, the result would be a simple absence—a void. And that is not what we find.

6.2 Eros Transfigured

That flesh is damaged and its caresses therefore often concupiscent (1.4, 6.1) seems clear enough, both to those who've been catechized by the grammar of Christian thought and to those who haven't. It's hard to doubt that the barrier between the caress and the wound is thin and porous, and that there are many cases in which the two seem, and are, inextricable. Damage in this sense is at least common. But is it universal? Is it the case, as claimed (6.1), that every actual caress, *post lapsum*, is also a wound? This seems unlikely. Aren't there at least some pure and simple caresses that neither intend a wound nor leave one?

There are two trajectories to follow in thinking about this. One, broadly empirical, is to consider some putative cases of caresses that involve no wounds, prescinding in doing so, so far as is possible for a Christian thinker, from the use of explicitly Christian categories. The second, specifically and explicitly Christian, is to consider the caresses of the natal flesh of Jesus (2.1) in order to see what they show about the pure, non-wounding caress. If there are any such caresses outside paradise and heaven, that's where they're to be found.

To the first: Are there, at first blush, non-wounding caresses that give and receive nothing but the gift of flesh? Consider the caress exchanged by mother and infant when the child sucks at the breast. Assume, too, that the mother and infant are not unusually disordered in their affections or their flesh—that, say, the infant is two months old and healthily growing, that the mother is no more than usually exhausted or unwell, that each is affectionately bonded (to the degree that a two-month-old can be said to have affections) to the other, and that a mutually satisfying and pleasurable rhythm of feeding and eating has been established. Some actual cases, probably, approximate this ideal. Don't we have here something like a pure caress, in which the only thing given is the reciprocal gift of flesh, and in which neither participant is performing the solipsistic expropriations characteristic of the concupiscent caress (6.1)? No. There is always, in the mother, some tincture of resentment at the demands made on her flesh by the infant, boredom at the repetitive and time-consuming nature of the act, eagerness for this feeding to be over and for the infant to be weaned, and fear that the infant is not flourishing as it should and that she is not giving it enough—milk, love, caresses, attention, and so forth. And, on the part of the infant there is always and inevitably solipsism, fear, and self-righteous aggression. Infants of two months, while they recognize the presence of those intimate with them (they do that even in the womb), do not acknowledge them as flesh (or persons) other than themselves. They are not yet even fully cognizant of the boundaries of their own flesh, and they recognize and respond to the flesh of others only insofar as it pleasures or pains theirs. They are not far in these respects from the ideal type of concupiscence, which is, from a Christian point of view, good evidence for the fact of the devastation, and for the presence of damage in the world independent of the sins committed by those suffering it. Infants exhibit also, when signalling their hunger in preparation for eating, all the usual signs of anger—Why aren't I being fed now, at once?—and fear—Perhaps this time my hunger won't be attended to? All these instances of damage on the part of the feeding couple coexist typically with their opposites: with deep affection, the exchange of the gift of flesh, and so on. The mother is given herself as mother in the exchange, as the infant is given itself as infant. Nevertheless, in even the most intimate, relaxed, and loving cases of the suckling caress, the mother wounds the infant and the infant the mother.

Or, consider the case of lovers, kissing open-mouthed, staring into the darkness of one another's pupils, each holding the bowl of the other's skull in cupped hands. They strain toward one another to feel the tongue deep in the mouth and the full extent of the other's flesh against their own, pressed hard. They pull back, together, so that they can look at and see one another. Aren't their caresses an instance of simple gift, of the flesh-constituting donation of their own flesh to the other?

—There is certainly that in them, all other things being equal. But why think there is only that? The lovers have in mind and under their hands and on their lips not only the other's flesh as something given, to be delighted in; but also the pleasure of their own flesh to which the other's must be made to yield and for which it must be staged—and in those ways treated not as the flesh it is but rather as the flesh it must be made into. And, there is in the mind and heart of each lover, and in their very flesh, the caresses of others, real or imagined, remembered or hoped for. No lover, not even the most naïve and virginal, makes love only to the beloved. And, necessarily, every embrace, every caress, is shadowed by the awareness of its end, of the lovers' sundering (cleaving both joins and separates, 3.1), and this inflects the caress of the moment with greed and desperation. There is also, even in the best of cases, a sense on the part of each lover, inchoate usually, that this, whatever is being done now, is not enough—that what's wanted from the lover's caress cannot fully be had from it. The Augustinian version of this point is that we are necessarily restless until we find rest in the LORD (*inquietum est cor nostrum donec requiescat in te*); the Shakespearean version is that love's appetites are infinite, while every act, and all of them together, is a slave to limit—which means that appetite is never satisfied by act, never satiable in that way. In this case, too, therefore—the case of the well-ordered lovers cleaving to none other than their beloved—there is wound in the caress. This is evident to all but the most romantically infatuated lovers.

Perhaps the best example in the devastated human sphere of the caress that doesn't wound is the gift of an organ, a part of one's own flesh transplanted into another's. If there is any expropriative solipsism here, any desire to make the caressed flesh into a creature of one's own, it must be minimal. That is guaranteed by the fact that the donor ordinarily doesn't know who the recipient is. Also, if any wounds to the flesh of the recipient occur because of the transplant, that isn't because of any intent on the part of the donor. The caress in this case—and it is an intimate one; one way to understand it might be to say that a separated part of the donor's flesh now lives in the recipient's, constantly reciprocally caressing and being caressed—is intended for healing and often has that result. But it is a strange example. It feels forced to call it a caress given by one human to another, and that is mostly because when my kidney is removed from me, it's no longer part of my flesh, not a separated part of that flesh but, rather, a piece of flesh temporarily (while in transit) with its own life (1.3). When the kidney that was mine takes up residence in your flesh, it can be understood either as alien flesh now living in benevolent symbiosis with yours; or as, now, a constituent of your flesh. There are advantages to both ways of thinking. But it is odd, and implausible, to say that when my kidney is well seated in you I am caressing you. And if, as is probable, this is the best example that can be found of an undamaged, non-wounding human caress here below, we have strong support for the view that it is very difficult to find an example of any such thing. Broadly empirical study of human caresses yields the conclusion that they're arranged on a continuum of the more to the less damaged, but that none is damage-free.

Perhaps, however, the natal flesh of Jesus can provide a sense of what the simple caress exchanged between humans might be like. If it can, it will also show what the caresses of those whose flesh is cleaved to his are like when they act in a way conformable to what they became when they were baptized. I assume as axiomatic here, in accord with the fundamental grammar of Christianity, that the incarnate LORD is free from sin, inherited or performed, and that when his flesh is damaged, that is because, for providential purposes, he permits it to be. It is not because he is subject to damage (2.2).

Jesus's natal flesh is very often caressed and rather less often initiates caresses. Sometimes it, or something close to it such as his clothing, is touched by someone without invitation; sometimes he's pressed by the flesh of others in crowds; he's circumcised, baptized, hugged, has his feet anointed, is kissed, is bound and whipped and crucified, washes feet, caresses children, and heals the flesh of others by touch, sometimes using, as he does so, leakages from his own body (2.1). The caresses Jesus gives and receives in his natal flesh, as they're shown in Scripture, have two purposes. The first is to heal. This is sometimes done without touch, at a distance; but more often by means of, or with the accompaniment of, a caress, as in the case of Jairus's daughter, who is awakened from a seeming death by the touch of Jesus's hand; or in the case of the man born blind, who is given sight when Jesus spits on the ground, makes mud with his saliva and the dust from the ground, and smears the mud on the blind man's eyes—a double caress, with spit and fingers. The second purpose for Jesus's caresses, given and received, is to show something: in the case of his circumcision that he is a Jew, that his flesh is Jewish flesh; in the case of his baptism, that he is, in the flesh, the Son of the Father; in the case of the sinful woman who anoints his feet and bathes them with her tears and dries them with her hair, the texture of the relations between forgiveness and faith. And so on.

In all cases, Jesus's caresses are prevenient gifts. They give life to those who receive them, typically by returning their flesh to them, previously damaged and now whole. This is a recapitulation of the LORD's original act of creation out of nothing. That act gave creatures the gift of being, and to living creatures the gift of life, which is exactly the gift of flesh; that the gift was given out of nothing, where (and when) there was nothing from which it was or could have been made, shows its prevenience with perfect clarity, as well as the fact that the flesh so brought into being doesn't merit the gift. Merits accrue, when they do, consequent upon existence, not as precondition for existence. Jesus's healing caresses can also be understood as a type of baptism: they're acts that show, in what they do and how they're done, what the baptismal touch effects. That touch—the touch of the LORD given in the name of the LORD—transfigures the flesh touched by the LORD by cleaving it to the very one who touches it (3.1), and it does this not by destroying what it touches in order then to make something new, *ex nihilo*, but rather by taking what's already there, the good flesh given in creation (good, but now damaged), and making it a new creature: *si quis ergo in Christo, nova creatura; vetera transierunt, ecce, facta sunt nova*— if, then, anyone's in Christ, they're a new creature; the old things are gone, and look, the new have been made. Jesus's caresses in his natal flesh give newness to those he touches in just this way. What Jesus's natal caresses lack is any thread of expropriation or spoliation; and they never use force. It's not quite right to say that Jesus's natal flesh is without need for fleshly touch. He needed Mary's womb-caress, for example, and her breasts and milk, and the ordinary touches of others as he grew in wisdom and understanding. But he needed these for providential reasons (2.2), not, as we do, to provide for a lack. That's why his caresses are absent any possibility of solipsistic expropriation driven by lack.

The caresses offered and received by Christian flesh are transfigured into likeness with those given and received by Jesus's natal flesh. Being cleaved to that flesh (also to the risen and ascended flesh), Christians are given the gift of being able, to the degree that they're comfortable with and conformed to the one they're cleaved to, to offer caresses to others that escape the violence of expropriative solipsism. Those caresses, the LORD's caresses in our Christian hands, participate in the LORD's creation *ex nihilo*: when we offer and receive them, we bring into being something of a kind previously absent, which is to say a beloved. Beloveds are made by being loved; fleshly beloveds require fleshly love; and when that fleshly love is given as love, without violent expro-priation, then, *ecce, facta sunt nova*—look, the new things have been made, and the new things are beloveds. This possibility is the clearest instance we have of what being Jesus-cleaved does. It's not that Christians have left behind the ordinary violence of the devastated caress; it's certainly not that every Christian caress is fully participant in the LORD's kiss, fully and without corruption a giver of life; but it is that these things are now possible where before they were not; and it is that as Christians increase in holiness, one mark of their doing so is that their caresses' desperation, avid concupiscence, and solipsistic expro-priation are attenuated. The caress that also wounds can't be completely left behind before the resurrection. But what caresses that don't wound are like can be seen in the lives of those whose actions rarely speak against the LORD to whom they are cleaved.

6.3 Celibacy and Virginity

Christianity has a long history of advocating the condition of virginity and the practice of celibacy, and of elevating them above their opposites. Sometimes, this advocacy has taken extreme forms: the tradition isn't lacking in those who've thought and said that Christians ought to stop copulating altogether. And while that proved, after the fourth century or so, to be a position rejected by mainstream Christianity, the thought that there's something profoundly good about celibacy and virginity remains vigorous among Catholic and Or-thodox Christians, even if less so among Protestants—who show in this, more clearly than in any other way, their distance from mainstream Christianity. Celibacy and virginity, at the very least, tend to be depicted by the tradition as a practice and a condition peculiarly appropriate to Christian flesh. Celibates and virgins, according to this view, show in their celibacy and virginity a mode of intimacy with Jesus that indicates more fully than do the fleshly lives of the non-celibate and of those who aren't virgins what it's like to be cleaved to Jesus. That much is clear enough. It's much less clear, however, what celibacy and virginity amount to, and, because of that lack of clarity, there's significant dis-agreement within the tradition about what each entails.

I'll take a stipulative line to clear up some of the confusion. To be celibate (adjective, from Latin *caelibatus*) means to abstain, for some period, from cop-ulation. To be a celibate (noun, from Latin *caelebs*) means to be one who so abstains. According to this understanding, men and women can each, indifferently, be celibate; it also means that you can be celibate for a short while (this week) or a long time (the rest of your life). And it doesn't require, though it's compatible with, the taking of vows or entry into a particular state of life. Celibacy can be accidental, casual, enforced, vowed, and so on; its mark is simply the absence in the life of a celibate of a particular caress, that of copulation. For as long as the absence continues, life is marked by celibacy; when the absence ceases, so does celibacy.

What, more exactly, is copulation, the caress whose absence constitutes celibacy and whose occurrence ends it? Again, stipulation is necessary: English, like the other languages known to me, is relaxed and inventive in its sexual lexicon, and every verb ("to fuck," "to copulate," "to have sex," "to sleep with," "to know," and so on) in this area resists precision and technical definition, whether by euphemism or metaphorical extension. So, stipulatively (but in broad accord with the moral-theological tradition), I'll take "copulation" to mean the ejaculation of semen by a male human being into the vagina of a female human being. Such a caress requires, therefore, two people, one male and one female, and a particular kind of fleshly exchange between them. It doesn't require anything else: not the intent to procreate, not pregnancy as result, not love, not affection, not marriage—nothing but a penis and a vagina and an ejaculation. That's the caress incompatible with celibacy, the caress the occurrence of which brings celibacy to an end, and which vowed celibates renounce and abstain from. A virgin, we can say, again stipulatively, is someone, male or female, who has never copulated. Copulation brings virginity to an end, even if it occurs only once. Celibacy can precede and follow copulation; virginity can only precede it. Neither is the same as chastity, which—again stipulatively—I'll take to mean engaging only in caresses appropriate to one's state of life. You need be neither virginal nor celibate in order to be chaste.

For Christians, Mary's flesh provides the paradigm of virginity. She, according to the doctrine that she is *semper virgo*, always virginal, never copulates. She conceives and gives birth, but without copulation; and her life subsequent to Jesus's birth includes no such caresses. Her ascended flesh, therefore, is virginal. There are difficulties with this view, of course, not least among which is that Scripture speaks of Jesus's *fratres*, which may seem to suggest that Mary copulated with Joseph later in her life. However those difficulties are resolved, so far as Christian doctrine is concerned, Mary was and is a virgin, which means at least that no man's penis ever ejaculated in her vagina. Jesus's natal flesh, too, is taken almost unanimously by the speculative theological tradition to be celibate from beginning to end and, therefore, virginal according to the understanding of the word in play here. It's worth noting that the affirmation of Mary's perpetual virginity, and of the virginity and celibacy of Jesus's flesh in all its stages (natal, resurrected, ascended), carries with it no entailments or even suggestions as to other kinds of caress they may have performed. It amounts to a single and simple denial: no copulation on the part of either.

Why, then, with the definitions provided and with the flesh of Jesus and Mary in mind, has Christianity tended so strongly to positively validate celibacy and virginity? There are many causes for this, the deepest among which is that copulation is implicated with procreation, and that procreation is an element in the economy of death. The connection between procreation (and other, non-sexual, modes of generation) and death is clear enough biologically, and even clearer theologically. Biologically, reproduction makes sense only where there's death. Organisms not subject to corruption and decay would, were they to re-produce, do something unnecessary, and something that would rapidly bring their own continued existence into question. We reproduce slowly by the stan-dards of most other living creatures, but even we, were we to procreate and not die other than by violence or accident, would soon fill the world. Generation is produced by death and leads to it, as every parent and every child knows. Pro-creative copulation without inevitable parental death makes as much sense as the practice of a healing art in a world without sickness. In neither case is there anything to remedy, and in neither case is it plausible that procreation or heal-ing would have come into existence. It is possible, I suppose, that procreation could be a feature of a world without death in the same way that a spandrel is a feature of Gothic architecture, which is to say as an epiphenomenon without function. But that is not the world we live in. In this world, the actual fallen and devastated world, procreative copulation goes with death, both causally (death is why it exists) and functionally (death is what it remedies).

Theologically, too, there's a strong case for thinking of procreative copula-tion as an element in the economy of death, and of Mary's virginity and Jesus's celibacy as marks of their separation from that economy—as givers of life-without-death rather than of life-predicated-upon-death. Jesus's flesh comes into being, in the temporal order, in the womb of a sinless woman (she is im-maculately conceived and doesn't commit sin subsequent to her conception), and is himself, because he is a double-natured divine-human person, without sin. In his flesh, he does not participate in the economy of death at all, and permits damage to his flesh, including his own death, for providential reasons only (2.2), not because he is subject to damage and death. Mary's agreement to conceive and bear Jesus virginally, and Jesus's own celibate life, resonate with and show exemption from death's dominion. Copulation, with or without consequent reproduction, would have resonated with and shown their complicity in the economy of death, and without, so far as my theological imagination takes me, any providential reason to make it appropriate. Therefore, Mary's virginity and Jesus's celibacy are elegantly appropriate to who they were. That's the pattern of reasoning and imagination that informs the broad Christian advocacy of the state of virginity and the practice of celibacy.

The position is formally like the one that informs the Christian position about fasting and eucharist (5.1, 5.3). The eucharist is life-giving food exempted entirely from the economy of slaughter with which all other food and eating is connected; fasting, as preparation for receiving the eucharist, participates in that exemption; and so fasting is something that Christian flesh does as an outflow of its cleaving to Jesus. As preparation for eating life it abstains from eating death. Celibacy is likewise appropriate for Christian flesh, whether as a temporary abstention from copulation or as a lifelong one. There has been, from time to time within the long tradition, both Western and Eastern, advocacy of temporary celibacy as preparation for receiving the eucharist (the Roman Catechism, promulgated after the Council of Trent, requires this), in very much the same way that fasting is required or recommended as preparation for receiving the eucharist. Catholic Christians are no longer required to abstain from copulation in this way, mostly because the Church now recommends frequent reception of the sacrament, which would make copulation effectively impossible for those who communicate frequently were preparatory abstinence required (fasting regulations were altered, though not abolished, for the same reason). But the pattern of reasoning remains: copulation is inseparable from the economy of death and has, therefore, a tensive relation with the eucharist, which belongs without remainder to the economy of life.

There's a broadly eschatological pattern of thought here. As in paradise, so in heaven, there won't be copulation because there won't be procreation. Jesus is recorded as speaking to one aspect of this in the twenty-second chapter of Matthew's Gospel, where he replies to a question from the Sadducees by saying, *in resurrectione enim neque nubent neque nubentur, sed sicut angeli in caelo*—for in the resurrection people are neither married nor given in marriage, but are like the angels in heaven. Scripture is less clear about the presence or absence of copulation in paradise before the fall, but the dominant traditional position, even if with many counter-voices, is that those texts, too, are best read as denying it, or at least as denying the procreative possibilities of copulation there. Christian flesh that lives celibately now, therefore, anticipates, in renouncing copulation, a condition in which we'll all share when resurrected. This thought contributes to the general adoption of celibacy by the religious orders, and to the eventual mandate of priestly celibacy in the West.

—But doesn't this understanding of copulation as participatory in the economy of death imply that there are no goods proper to the copulatory caress? Doesn't it also sit uneasily with the Catholic Church's current teaching on the goods and joys proper to marital copulation? Isn't it even the case that current Catholic moral theology, both speculative and magisterial, is moving away from understanding and depicting the celibate state as superior in any way to the copulatively-active married state? Hasn't the older hierarchical ordering of the celibate and married states been effectively left behind?

—There's something in all this. Catholic bishops, popes, and speculative theologians have, in the last several generations, had a good deal to say about the goods belonging to married and family life, including the goods of the copulative caress. Augustine, long before, had some things to say about this too. But none of that stands in any necessary tension with the line taken here. To observe that a particular pattern of action is inseparable from the economy of death doesn't suggest that it lacks all goods, and much less that it lacks all delights. Non-eucharistic eating is inseparable from that economy in this way, but is also replete with delights and goods. Copulation likewise: it is, when other conditions are as they should be, a delightful caress for both partners and contains many goods, including at least the forming of the copulating couple into a kind of intimacy that participates in that shared by Jesus with the Church and, sometimes, the bringing into being of children. These are real goods. Affirming them ought not blind us to the involvement, nonetheless, of copulation in death, and the performance of it, therefore, as participatory in that economy. To occlude either the goods or the lacks of the copulatory caress is a mistake; seeing both clearly shows copulation as a caress that should prompt both joy and lament among Christians. In this, too, it is like eating; and the response of Christian flesh to it should be of the same kind.

It's true, too, that the Church's teachers are less inclined than they once were to affirm that the celibate state, when intentional and lifelong, is more appropriate for Christian flesh than non-celibacy; and it's true that this conclusion doesn't follow from anything that's been said here. What does follow is that celibacy has goods in it that non-celibacy lacks, and that among those goods is anticipatory conformity of Jesus-cleaved flesh here below to resurrected flesh in heaven. But it may be, and probably is, that the celibate state carries with it lacks and dangers that non-celibates aren't subject to (pride at their superiority to the non-celibate is likely one), and if that's the case—a matter beyond the scope of this book; Augustine has some trenchant things to say about it in his treatise on virginity—then perhaps the best conclusion is that celibacy and non-celibacy are alike flawed goods for Christian flesh, and should alike prompt the characteristic response of Christian flesh to its own necessities (among which is that you're going to be celibate or not, like it or not), which is lament-tinged rejoicing.

There's another point to make about the copulatory caress, one that was also often made in premodern Christian moral theology, and which is less commonly made now, even though it remains true. It's that the copulatory caress is especially closely connected with concupiscently idolatrous fornication. That is, the passions connected with it are rarely, perhaps never, fully separate from a violent desire to expropriate the partner's flesh by making it, solipsistically, a wholly owned object for one's own gratification (6.1). There are many signs of this in the form of the caress itself. One is orgasm, which belongs to it for men and may accompany it for women. While people experience orgasm differently, and perhaps among these differences are some that differentiate, typically, women from men (the empirical literature on this question is complex and disputed), a widely shared characteristic of orgasm is the temporary obliteration of the flesh of the other as other. Orgasms, like sneezes and pains, tend to close the flesh's horizon in upon itself and thus to make the presence of the other at best ancillary and at worst irrelevant. The gift character of the fleshly caress is in part occluded by this closure, and while non-copulatory caresses may also involve orgasm, they're not defined by its necessity and are therefore less subject to it. And so the partial occlusion of the caress—its movement from caress to wound—is closer to the surface and deeper in the structure of the copulatory caress than is the case for most other caresses. Another sign of the connection between copulation and idolatrous fornication is the ease with which the copulatory caress is commercialized. It can be done without face-to-face or eye-to-eye or lip-to-lip connection, and between prostitutes and their clients it often is. Many other fleshly caresses are less easy to separate from the mutual gift of the flesh. And lastly, copulation is very often, perhaps ordinarily until recent times, treated instrumentally, principally as a means of making babies, which is an end extrinsic to the fleshly exchange of gifts. When a couple copulates with nothing but the end of procreation in view, they are by definition withholding their flesh from one another by making their caress subservient to a consequence that may or may not flow from it. This too is a kind of concupiscence, even if not so self-evidently an idolatrous one.

Neither celibacy nor virginity is required or commanded for Christian flesh: no fleshly gesture is, other than baptism and eucharist. The beauty of celibacy and virginity when they are practiced consists, first, in the participatory intimacy of virginal and celibate flesh, exactly in its celibacy and virginity, with the virginal celibacy of both Mary's and Jesus's flesh; and, second, in their prolepsis of the celibacy of all resurrected flesh. The strange condition of virginity and the alien practice of celibacy—strange and alien to most humans, both pagan and Jewish—can be given sense by Christians, and ought to be celebrated when encountered.

6.4 Forbidden Caresses

Are there particular caresses, particular skin-to-skin fleshly exchanges, forbidden to Christian flesh by precept or command? If so, what are they, and why are they forbidden? I'm not here concerned with caresses forbidden because of conditions extrinsic to the caress: you might have a caress placed off-limits to you because of positive laws in your jurisdiction (perhaps public kissing is illegal where you live; and strangling—a caress that is also a wound—is very likely to be), because of promises you've made (perhaps you've promised to copulate with only one person, or with none, and are therefore constrained from doing so with others), or because of local custom (perhaps the skin-to-skin of the handshake at first meeting is scandalously intimate where you live). There are always many conditions of that sort; every human society has strong norms, some explicit and some implicit, about which caresses are acceptable and performable, and which are not. I'm not here concerned with those constraints. I'm interested, rather, in whether there are caresses *malum in se* for Christian flesh, caresses therefore forbidden to Christians because of their very form, no matter what local laws, customs, or particular promises are also in play.

I've argued already that the LORD, in cleaving human flesh to Jesus, asks nothing of it and therefore obliges it, as flesh, to nothing (3.1, 3.2, 3.3). This is a controversial position among Christians. If it can be defended, it should apply here too, and its upshot is that no, there are no caresses forbidden to Christian flesh simply because of their form—or for any other reason. Rather, some caresses sit well with Christian flesh, and others less well. Christians learn to increase the frequency of the former and reduce the frequency of the latter not by attending to codes or precepts, but rather by attending to Jesus, the one to whose flesh they are already cleaved by gift. Codes framed in the imperative or subjunctive have their uses—as mnemonics, as diagnostics, and so forth. But they are not to be taken as encapsulating demands the LORD makes on Christian flesh because there are no such demands. The question then is: are there caresses whose form speaks strongly against Christian flesh, caresses that are, because of that, unlikely to be performed by the saints?

I'll approach this question by considering, briefly, three instances of caresses that often have been, and often still are, depicted as forbidden to Christian flesh, and in each case showing that they need not be so depicted—that there is nothing in their form that makes them per se inappropriate for Christian flesh, even if each of them has, in its own characteristic fashion, concupiscent aspects and tendencies. The three are: masturbation, cunnilingus, and sodomy. I begin by presenting, as counterpoint, the copulative caress as performed by those sacramentally married. This is a caress that only marginal voices in the Christian tradition think of as forbidden; most Christians now, including those who formulate Catholic doctrine on these matters, understand that caress to be a real good and (sometimes) an actual delight, something entirely appropriate to Christian flesh. Contrasting the other three caresses to it will show something important about what is appropriate for Christian flesh in them and what is not.

I've already discussed the copulative caress in the context of celibacy (6.3), and here restate the definition given there: copulation is the ejaculation of semen by a male human being into the vagina of a female human being. That is the form of the caress, the action in which it essentially consists. Its principal goods are two: it can intertwine the lives of those who share it in ways analogous to the fleshly intertwining in which it consists, linking them over the course of a life so that mutual support and sacrifice of self for the good of the other are deepened and enhanced; and it can produce offspring, human creatures who otherwise would not exist. It need do neither of these things, of course: it can be brutal, violent, solipsistic, expropriative, and, in general, idolatrous (6.1); and it can be performed over the course of a life without ever producing offspring. Even when procreation does occur, it ordinarily does so in only a tiny fraction of copulations. When, from a Christian point of view, the copulative caress is performed by those who've been sacramentally married, it is given a possibility unavailable when done by those not sacramentally married. That possibility is that it can participate in and image the love of Jesus for the Church. This transfigures copulation for Christian flesh; when the Church discovered—and it took a long time to do so—that marriage could be part of the sacramental life of Christians, the copulative aspects of flesh's eros were transfigured (6.2). But even in this case, it isn't that all copulations by the sacramentally married participate identically, with equally deep ingression, in Jesus's love for the Church. They all fail to do so to some degree, and some fail dramatically and deeply, showing on their surface and in their depths expropriative idolatry as solipsistic and violent as anything evident in the copulations of those not sacramentally married. The sacrament of baptism makes Christian flesh, and the sacrament of marriage marries Christian flesh; but neither makes everything done thereafter conformable to what's been created. Christian spouses can rape one another and baptized Christians can murder one another. Holiness is not equally distributed even within the sacramental economy; the flesh isn't transfigured all at once and without remainder.

With this view of copulation by the sacramentally married in the background, as counterpoint, what about masturbation? In what respects does the form of this caress speak against Christian flesh, and in what respects for it? Masturbation is a self-caress: the intentional stimulation of one's own genitals for pleasure, and in some cases for orgasm. It is very widely practiced by humans, and by some other mammals; only a tiny proportion of humans has never done it, and it is done at almost every stage of life, from infancy to old age. Christian critiques of it, of which there are many, typically understand it as an inadequate substitute for copulation. On this view, what's wrong with it is that it uses the capacity for genital pleasure, whether orgasmic or otherwise, in an inappropriate way. That capacity, extreme forms of the critique may say, serves one purpose only, which is copulation, as described. To separate it from that context and use it for some other purpose—in the case of masturbation, for pleasure—is, according to this line of thought, always inappropriate for Christian flesh, and the extent to which it is done is the extent to which those who do it have not become comfortable with being cleaved to Christ. Those whose cleaving is comfortable and habitual don't do it: their flesh's capacity for genital pleasure is reserved to copulation and they find masturbation, therefore, when it occurs to them, absurd, ridiculous, unbecoming.

This line of reasoning, if it can be dignified with that label, tends to get more exercised by masturbation that leads to ejaculation than by masturbation that doesn't and, therefore, to be more exercised by male than female masturbation. This is because masturbation is assessed in terms of its likeness to copulation, and that likeness is more evident when ejaculation occurs than when it doesn't. If ejaculation's only proper context is copulative, then it follows at once that masturbatory ejaculation must be at least inappropriate for Christian flesh. But there is no compelling need to think of masturbation as a damaged or inadequate substitute for copulation, and much that speaks against such a view. Humans masturbate when they are too young to copulate or procreate or ejaculate, and when they are too old to procreate or ejaculate. They masturbate, too, when they have an active copulatory life. To think that all genital pleasure serves copulatory purposes and should be restricted to them is a little like thinking that all vocalization serves the purpose of communicating thought: it's a view largely insulated from empirical study and from theological analysis of the excessiveness and range of human capacities in these areas. Our genital pleasures include copulation, certainly, but also masturbation, fellatio, sodomy, cunnilingus, and much more. Our vocalizations include the communication of thought, certainly, but also singing, grunting, humming, exclamation, onomatopoeic imitation, and much more. And theologically, we should expect what we find, which is that our fleshly appetites and capacities generally vastly exceed a single purpose or end: eating isn't just for nourishment, and clothing isn't just for protecting the flesh. The LORD gives excessively to us in our flesh, which is a matter for delight; and the appetites and range of our fleshly capacities for pleasure are therefore also excessive, which is also a matter for delight. Criticizing masturbation as a damaged approximation of copulation denies these points, and is risible on its face.

—But isn't there a more subtle and more convincing Christian critique of masturbation than this? Can't it be said—don't Christians often say—that masturbation tends toward, or just is, a concupiscent caress (6.1), one concerned solipsistically with self-pleasure, with the staging of one's own flesh as a pleasure ground, and therefore a caress separated from the gift of the flesh as flesh? Can't it at least be said that genital pleasures require a partner if they are to belong to the gift economy? This position doesn't require the thought that masturbation is to be assessed solely in terms of its relation to copulation.

—This is a more subtle position, and one with something to be said for it. It's certainly the case that masturbation tends toward solipsism; its deformation is to become exactly a habit of self-gratification in which genital pleasure is turned only toward one's own flesh, and in which the flesh of others figures only as a spectacle, an imagined possession which is, like all possessions, entirely responsive to the will of the owner and therefore incapable of offering real gifts. Yes. This is also why masturbation often (but not necessarily and not always) involves the use of pornographic images or imaginings. When masturbation moves along these trajectories, or when these elements, always present in it to some degree, become dominant, it is to that extent concupiscent and contradictory to what Christian flesh is. But these deformities aren't the only things present in masturbation. Self-pleasuring, like soliloquizing, is also an instrument by which masturbators (soliloquists) give their flesh to themselves as flesh. The discovery of the flesh's capacities for genital pleasure, up to and including orgasm but by no means limited to that, is in part one that must be given by oneself to oneself. Infants suck their fingers and play with their genitals; children and adolescents and adults may, and sometimes do, give themselves to themselves as pleasure-capable flesh in much the same way that, by talking to themselves, they nuance and burnish, by self-gift, their capacities for speech. Christian flesh need find nothing tensive in this.

Masturbation is always in part concupiscent, always in part avidly and expropriatively greedy for gratification. Because of that, it's always capable of moving the masturbator away from Jesus and toward the lack that is self-possession. But in this it is not unlike copulation, even the copulation of the sacramentally married. It cannot, therefore, be judged contradictory to Christian flesh on that ground. Rather, it should be judged an ordinary part of the repertoire of caresses that belongs to Christian flesh here below in the devastation.

This pattern of reasoning is important, and can be applied, with modifications, to the other caresses about to be discussed. At its heart is a rejection of the idea that there are just two kinds of caress, one *malum in se*, always and everywhere inappropriate in its very form for Christian flesh; and the other undamaged and beautiful, always appropriate and never to be lamented. Once that dichotomy is left behind, on the principal ground that no kind of caress is, since the fall, exempt from damage, and, correspondingly, that no kind of caress is, since the fall, damage without remainder, the question changes. It becomes: What are the goods in this kind of caress, whether in its form or in its observed or conjectured effects, and what are its deformities? The answer is always that it has both characteristic deformities and characteristic beauties.

What then—our second example—of cunnilingus, understood as the caress of a woman's genitals by someone's (whether the someone is male or female is irrelevant for the moment) tongue? This caress, too, has sometimes been criticized and placed under the ban by Christians because it is taken to be a deceptive or otherwise inadequate simulacrum of copulation. If female genital pleasure, and the caress of the female genitals, is reserved to copulation, having that as its only end and context, then it at once follows that other modes of caress involving female genitalia are improper, whether for Christian flesh or otherwise. But this reason for judging cunnilingus inappropriate for Christian flesh can be rejected rapidly with the same pattern of reasoning as given above for masturbation: there is no good reason, theological or empirical, to think of cunnilingus in this way. It may serve as propaedeutic to copulation, but it need not, and often does not; and it is not, by itself, in its form, copulative or pro-creative. And the second pattern of reasoning used to criticize masturbation—that it has a particular and marked tendency to solipsistic expropriation of the flesh, and is to that extent insulated from gift-exchange, has no purchase here. In cunnilingus there are two people involved, and there is genuine fleshly exchange. It is subject to deformities, no doubt; but there's no reason to think it more so or differently so than copulation. Cunnilingus, too, then, can reasonably be regarded as potentially, and sometimes actually (how often actually is a matter for empirical study), a caress that can give the gift of flesh and that can intertwine the lives of those who exchange it into a pattern deeply resonant with that evident in Jesus's relation to the Church.

Sodomy is our third example. This, let's say, is the penetration of someone's anal cavity by someone's erect penis, followed by ejaculation therein. The sex of the one performing the penetration is necessarily male, but that of the one being penetrated is left undetermined by the definition. There are current in English both broader and narrower understandings of the word; it's often extended to include bestiality, for instance, and sometimes restricted to male-male human acts. I'll consider it in the intermediate sense given. Christian criticisms of this act are by now familiar: what's wrong with it is that it's a damaged, inadequate, and deceptive form of copulation, whether performed by a man upon a man or a man upon a woman. These criticisms are more intense and more frequent among Christians because there is arguably some scriptural basis for them, and because the sodomitic caress has more immediate formal similarities to the copulative caress than do masturbation or cunnilingus. But the same rebuttal of these criticisms applies here as was given in those cases. There is no good empirical evidence for the claim that sodomy is a simulacrum of copulation, and no good theological argument that it should be so regarded. Opposite-sex couples who engage in sodomy (and most sodomy occurs in such a context) don't, typically, refrain from copulation, any more than do those that kiss or perform cunnilingus; the sodomitic caress may be performed for its own sake, independently of any connection to copulation; or it may be performed as part of a repertoire of caresses, to which both it and copulation belong. For same-sex sodomites, copulation isn't possible. For them, sodomy may or may not be important in the repertoire of flesh-giving caresses shared, and may or may not be articulated with other caresses. Variation is wide on all these points, as it also is on the extent to which sodomitic caresses contribute to a mutually supportive intertwined life of a kind intimate with Jesus's love for the Church. Often they do and often they don't, just as is the case with the copulative caress.

One of the difficulties in much Christian—and especially Catholic—speculative theology about fleshly caresses is an overestimation of the importance of the copulative caress, and a concomitant over-assimilation of other caresses to it. This overestimation is unnecessary, and no part of the deposit of faith. The copulative caress is one among many, and neither the most common nor the most profound. The intimacy evident in the eye-to-eye gaze and the lip-to-lip kiss is in many respects deeper than that evident in copulation (6.2, 6.3, 6.4); and the extent to which non-copulative caresses bind lives together as Jesus binds the Church to himself is an empirical question, not one to which doctrine can give a direct answer. The same is true of the question—which is *the* question so far as Christian flesh is concerned—about which caresses speak against being cleaved to Jesus and which speak for it. Nor can answers to that question be read from simple observation of the form of the caress. They require knowledge of context and formation and effect over time, as is also the case for assessments of which forms of eating or clothing are scandalously or idolatrously meretricious (4.6, 5.6).

A final comment is necessary on same-sex caresses, since this is a matter that exercises the churches considerably. If we abjure the category of the sexual and instead consider caresses in their formal and gorgeous variety, and if we consider caresses in terms of the extent to which they're concupiscently expropriative and therefore solipsistic, then the difficulty vanishes. The point isn't the sex, or gender, of those exchanging caresses; the point is the extent to which the caresses they exchange comport well with their condition as Jesus-cleaved. And that isn't determined by the sex or gender of the participants. There's neither theological nor empirical reason to think so.

—But doesn't this position directly contradict the ordinary and universal magisterial teaching of the Catholic Church on homosexuality? Doesn't that teaching say that homosexual desires, acts, and habits are intrinsically disordered?

—So, generally speaking, it does. What's offered here is not a contradiction of that teaching, but rather a *dubium*, a doubt about whether in its usual acceptation that teaching is right. The doubt works on two levels: first, by trying to see what can be said about particular fleshly exchanges without assimilating them to, or considering them in terms of, the copulative caress; and second, by opening the way for interpretive work on magisterial teachings of this kind. What is a homosexual caress? What a homosexual tendency? What a homosexual desire? These two kinds of doubt are speculative; considering them might produce further theological thought about these matters, and might also, over time, provoke doctrinal development with respect to them.

6.5 Caressing Jesus

Skin is the flesh's integument; flesh is given its haptic constitution paradigmatically by skin-to-skin touch, which is to say by the caress. We Christians are cleaved to the flesh of Jesus in baptism, and so our flesh is his: we are his limbs and members. When we caress Christian flesh and are caressed by it, then, we caress and are caressed by Jesus. That's one way of doing it. We also caress his ascended flesh directly when we receive it in the eucharist: we ingest and digest it. That's another way of doing it. Each is an intimately real caress. But neither is enough because both are veiled, the one by the skin of human creatures who aren't the ascended LORD, and the other by the appearance and the feel of bread. We want more than veiled caresses. If you're my beloved, the one who's given me by way of your caresses the unparalleled gift of being a beloved, and, therefore, a lover, I want to touch you unveiled. I don't want clothes or other human beings or the accidents of bread to be what it seems to me I'm touching. I want it to seem to me that what I touch is you, skin to skin, unveiled. I want that from and with Jesus, too, more, in fact, than with any human beloved; and I want it with any human beloved only because I want it with him. The monstrosity of my desires for human flesh other than my own is a direct outflow of the fact that the flesh I want, the only flesh that can satisfy that monstrosity, is Jesus's. When I can caress him and be caressed by him, in his ascended flesh, unveiled, with full and unmediated intimacy, what I seek now in copulation, in orgasm, in the kiss, in the desperate clutch for the other's flesh, will at last be given. My skin will be touched by his, and his by mine. That's part of what the resurrection means: receiving Jesus's caresses.

This may sound overheated. Most contemporary Christians in Europe and North America are made uneasy by language like this. They tend to deny that they want to touch Jesus or be touched by him. Isn't it enough to look and see, they say? Isn't that what Scripture commends to us—that we'll see and know the LORD as we are known? Why place all this emphasis on touch? Won't we then be beyond all that? Well, no, we won't. The characteristic doctrine of Christianity, the assertion that makes it not Platonism and not, really, anything but itself, is that we shall be resurrected in the flesh, the selfsame flesh that we have now (though the meaning of "selfsame" remains deeply obscure), there to be in the company of the other saints resurrected before the face and within the reach of the ascended LORD and his mother. The saints in heaven before the resurrection, existing discarnately as separated souls, can see and know the LORD already, *sine carne*. We expect, finally, more than that: we expect whatever it is that the resurrection of the flesh adds to the capacity for sight and understanding, and that can only be touch. We expect the LORD's caress, skin to skin. That is the culmination of the Christian life. That is when Christian flesh becomes fully itself, unveiled to Jesus and with Jesus unveiled to it, in full tactile intimacy with its LORD.

WORKS CONSULTED

My text of reference for Scripture is that of the *Nova Vulgata* as given in the second typical edition published at Rome in 1986. All scriptural quotations in Latin are taken from that text, and all scriptural quotations in English are my renderings of the New Vulgate's Latin. This book is otherwise light in quotation from the work of others, though there are many allusions to, echoes of, and thoughts provoked by such work, some of which I'm aware of. The list that follows, ordered alphabetically, is of works I recall having read and been stimulated by (as often negatively as positively) while preparing for and writing this book. I indicate them in the language I read them in, which is usually the language in which they were composed. I don't provide complete publication details for these works—the Web makes that supererogatory—but I do provide a parenthetical date for first publication, usually imprecise for premodern works. There are no doubt many works that have shaped my thought on the matters I address in this book that don't appear in this list because of my forgetfulness, and still more I would have benefitted from reading had time and energy allowed.

Agamben, Giorgio. *L'aperto* (2002).
Agamben, Giorgio. *Il Regno e la Gloria* (2007).
Agamben, Giorgio. *Pilato e Gesú* (2013).
Anderson, Gary A. *The Genesis of Perfection* (2001).
Anidjar, Gil. *Blood* (2014).
Aquinas, Thomas. *Summa Contra Gentiles* (13th c.).
Aquinas, Thomas. *Summa Theologiae* (13th c.).
Augustine. *De bono coniugali* (5th c.).
Augustine. *De civitate Dei* (5th c.)
Augustine. *De cura pro mortuis gerenda* (5th c.).
Augustine. *De sancta virginitate* (5th c.).

Augustine. *De trinitate* (5th c.)

Banks, Russell. *Lost Memory of Skin* (2011).

Bennett, Jana Marguerite. *Water Is Thicker than Blood* (2008).

Berlant, Lauren, and Lee Edelman. *Sex, Or the Unbearable* (2014).

Bernanos, Georges. *Monsieur Ouine* (1943).

Brague, Rémi. *Au moyen du Moyen Âge* (2006).

Brock, Sebastian. "Clothing Metaphors" (1981).

Burke, Cormac. "A Postscript to the *Remedium Concupiscentiae*" (2006).

Burke, Cormac. *The Theology of Marriage* (2015).

Burrus, Virginia, et al. *Seducing Augustine* (2010).

Bynum, Caroline Walker. *The Resurrection of the Body in Western Christianity 200–1336* (1995).

Bynum, Caroline Walker. *Christian Materiality* (2011).

Cahall, Perry. "Saint Augustine on Conjugal Love and Divine Love" (2004).

Carson, Anne. *Eros, the Bittersweet* (1998).

Carson, Anne. *Decreation* (2005).

Cary, Phillip. *Outward Signs* (2008).

Cavell, Stanley, et al. *Philosophy and Animal Life* (2008).

Classen, Constance, ed. *The Book of Touch* (2005).

Coakley, Sarah. *God, Sexuality, and the Self* (2013).

Coakley, Sarah. *The New Asceticism* (2015).

Coetzee, J. M. *Disgrace* (1999).

Coetzee, J. M. *Elizabeth Costello* (2003).

Coetzee, J. M., et al. *The Lives of Animals* (1999).

Cooper, Adam G. *The Body in St. Maximus the Confessor* (2005).

Crisp, Oliver D. *God Incarnate* (2009).

DeYoung, Rebecca Konyndyk. *Glittering Vices* (2009).

Dickens, Charles. *Little Dorrit* (1855–1857).

Dodaro, Robert, ed. *Remaining in the Truth of Christ* (2014).

Fairlie, Henry. *The Seven Deadly Sins Today* (1978).

Falque, Emmanuel. *Triduum Philosophique* (2015).

Farley, Margaret. *Just Love* (2006).

Farrow, Douglas. *Ascension Theology* (2011).

Field, Tiffany. *Touch* (2014).

Gschwandtner, Christina M. "Corporeality, Animality, Bestiality" (2012).

Harper, Kyle. *From Shame to Sin* (2013).

Hart, David Bentley. *The Beauty of the Infinite* (2003).

Hart, David Bentley. *Atheist Delusions* (2009).

Hart, David Bentley. *The Experience of God* (2013).

Henry, Michel. *Incarnation* (2000).

Hunter, David G. *Marriage, Celibacy, and Heresy in Ancient Christianity* (2007).

Ind, Jo. *Memories of Bliss: God, Sex, and Us* (2003).

Jordan, Mark D. *The Invention of Sodomy in Christian Theology* (1997).

Jordan, Mark D. *The Ethics of Sex* (2002).

Jordan, Mark D. *Recruiting Young Love* (2011).

Joyce, George Hayward. *Christian Marriage* (1933).

Jütte, Robert. *A History of the Senses* (2005).

Kearney, Richard, and Brian Treanor, ed. *Carnal Hermeneutics* (2015).

Kelly, Anthony J. *God Is Love* (2012).

Kelly, Anthony J. *Upward* (2014).

Kleinberg, Aviad. *7 Deadly Sins* (2008).

Leigh-Fermor, Patrick. "Gluttony" (1962).

Linden, David J. *Touch: The Science of Hand, Heart, and Mind* (2015).

MacIntyre, Alasdair. "What Is A Human Body?" (2006).

Madigan, Kevin J. *The Passions of Christ in High-Medieval Thought* (2007).

Madigan, Kevin J. and Jon D. Levenson. *Resurrection* (2008).

Marion, Jean-Luc. *De surcroît* (2002).

Marion, Jean-Luc. *Le phénomène érotique* (2003).

Marion, Jean-Luc. *Au lieu de soi* (2008).

McCarthy, Cormac. *Suttree* (1979).

McCarthy, Cormac. *Blood Meridian* (1985).

Miller, Geoffrey David. "Trying to Fix the Family Tree of Jesus" (2009).

Montagu, Ashley. *Touching* (3rd ed. 1986).

Morgan, C. E. *All the Living* (2009).

Morgan, C. E. *The Sport of Kings* (2016).

Oakes, Edward T. *Infinity Dwindled to Infancy* (2011).

Paterson, Mark. *The Senses of Touch* (2007).

Pépin, Jean. "Saint Augustin et le symbolisme néoplatonicien de la vêture" (1954).

Peterson, Erik. "Theologie des Kleides" (1934).

Prose, Francine. "Gluttony" (1993).

Pruss, Alexander. *One Body* (2013).

Quasten, Johannes. "The Garment of Immortality" (1966).

Rees, Geoffrey. *The Romance of Innocent Sexuality* (2011).

Richardson, Sarah S. *Sex Itself: The Search for Male and Female in the Human Genome* (2013).

Rivera, Mayra. *Poetics of the Flesh* (2015).

Rogers, Eugene F. *Sexuality and the Christian Body* (1999).

Sigurdson, Ole. *Heavenly Bodies* (2016).

Silverman, Kaja. *Flesh of My Flesh* (2009).

Silverman, Kaja. *The Miracle of Analogy* (2015).

Smith, Mark M. *Sensing the Past* (2007).

Steinberg, Leo. *The Sexuality of Christ in Renaissance Art and in Modern Oblivion* (2nd ed. 1996).

Taylor, Gabrielle. *Deadly Vices* (2006).

Tertullian. *De carne Christi* (3rd c.).

Tertullian. *De resurrectione mortuorum* (3rd c.).

Traina, Cristina L. H. *Erotic Attunement* (2011).

Trevor, William. "Gluttony" (1993).

Updike, John. "Lust" (1993).

Ward, Graham. "The Displaced Body of Jesus Christ" (1999).

Webb, Stephen. *Jesus Christ, Eternal God* (2012).

Weinandy, Thomas. *In the Likeness of Sinful Flesh* (1993).

Williams, Rowan. "The Body's Grace" (2002).

Winner, Lauren F. *Real Sex* (2005).

Winner, Lauren F. *Wearing God* (2015).

Yanagihara, Hanya. *The People in the Trees* (2013).

Yanagihara, Hanya. *A Little Life* (2015).

INDEX

Abattoir, 12, 117, 126. *See also* Concupiscence

Aging, 7; of Jesus, 36, 38–39

Appetite, 21–22, 113–115, 129, 141

Aquinas, Thomas, 114

Augustine, 93, 104, 136, 137

Babies, 20, 55, 75, 84, 138, 99, 124, 128. *See also* Infants

Ban, 67, 70–77, 79, 96, 99, 105–106, 138–145

Baptism: as caressing, 73; and Christian flesh, 59; and clothing, 83–86, 88; as fleshly gift, 73; Jesus's, 32, 42; Jesus's healing touch as, 131; and nakedness, 84, 98; relation to Eucharist, 51–52, 59, 120; as sacrament of cleaving, 51; and sex difference, 92–96; as toggle concept, 59

Baptismal garment, 59, 91–92, 110

Baptized flesh, 29, 58–60, 85, 91

Biblical texts, 2, 31–32, 36–37, 40, 41–43, 44–49, 52–53, 63–65, 70, 71–72, 73, 74, 86–88, 91, 92, 104, 105 109, 117. *See also* Mary Magdalene; Song of Songs; Thomas the Apostle.

Body, 2–9, 12–19, 58–59, 63–65; of Mary, 34, 53–54

Boundaries, spatial and temporal 12–20, 128; commensal, 129. *See also* Skin.

Buddhism, the Buddha, 1, 11, 24, 65

Caress, 5, 6, 9, 20–25, 35, 55, 74, 75, 123–146; baptismal, 73; cleaving and, 60–61, 67–69, 75; Jesus's received, 76; lingual,

of the Eucharist, 50–51, 55; related to wounds, 67, 74, 75, 76, 77

Celibacy, 132–135

Children, childhood, 20–25, 59, 62, 74–76, 128; of Ugolino, 111–113. *See also* Baby; Infant.

Chrismation, 59

Church, the, 2, 34, 77, 93 120, 136, 140, 144–145

Cleaving, 51, 60–78, 84–85, 100, 108, 128–135

Clothing, 79–101; badging, 80–81, 90–92, 94; enhancing fleshly powers, 80; necessity of, 90; ornament, 81; protective, 80.

Clothing, liturgical, 89–92; baptismal, 83–86; priestly, 91, 93

Commensality, 115, 118–121

Commercialization, 22, 69, 137

Concupiscence, 124–126, 128, 132, 138, 141

Contronym, 61–62

Copulation, 21–24, 133–146

Corpse, 5, 19, 25, 39, 58, 104, 108, 125–127; continues to contribute to the economy of death, 104; Jesus's, 13, 30; prepared for burial, 82

Creation out of nothing, 7–8, 131

Cunnilingus, 139, 143

Dante, 110–116

Death 1, 5, 9, 13, 18–19, 25–26, 39, 52, 56; economy of, and eating, 104–7; economy of, and procreation 134; and Garden of Eden story, 88–89; garments and, 86, 91; of Jesus' natal flesh, 28, 49, 85, 135

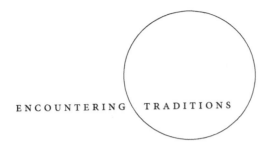

ENCOUNTERING TRADITIONS